MORE Letters from a Nut

MORE

Letters from a Nut

by

Ted L. Nancy

MORE INTRODUCTION BY
JERRY SEINFELD

BANTAM BOOKS New York London Toronto Sydney Auokland

MORE LETTERS FROM A NUT
A Bantam Book / April 1998

Library of Congress Cataloging-in-Publication Data

Nancy, Ted L.

More letters from a nut / by Ted L. Nancy;
more introduction by Jerry Seinfeld.

p.   cm.

ISBN 0-553-10958-8

1. Letters—Humor.   2. American wit and humor.   I. Title.

PN6131.N365   1998

813'.54—dc21   98-4923

CIP

Published simultaneously in the United States and Canada

Bantam Books are published by Bantam Books, a division of Bantam Doubleday Dell Publishing Group, Inc. Its trademark, consisting of the words "Bantam Books" and the portrayal of a rooster, is Registered in U.S. Patent and Trademark Office and in other countries. Marca Registrada. Bantam Books, 1540 Broadway, New York, New York 10036.

PRINTED IN THE UNITED STATES OF AMERICA

BVG   10 9 8 7 6 5

DEDICATED TO MY BEAUTIFUL PARENTS

When I said to my mother, "You thought I was going to
end up delivering pizzas for a living," she said,
"I was hoping."

ACKNOWLEDGMENTS

Thanks to Irwyn Applebaum, Katie Hall, Dan Strone, Pauline Hubert, and Jerry Seinfeld.

And to Phyllis Murphy, who said, "I still can't believe you wrote a letter to Fritos and they answered you!"

MORE INTRODUCTION

I fully admit that I bear a certain responsibility for the success and popularity of Ted Nancy. I discovered him, I promoted him, I allowed his name to be associated with mine. So I do accept the responsibility, but not the blame. I want it known that I never encouraged Mr. Nancy. I never asked him to further explore the dark inner passageways of his mind disease that is in full lurid bloom in this new book. I have decided I no longer want this micro-brained sociopath's ink on my hands.

In the beginning it all seemed like just a little mindless fun. "Hey, Dan," I said to Dan Strone, my good friend, trusted advisor, and super-agent of the William Morris Agency, "let's see if we can get this crazy guy's letters published as a book." Who knows, I thought, maybe people will get a kick out of it. How could I have not seen where it would lead? Why didn't I think? Am I so drunk on my own cool-medium charisma that I've totally lost my ability to discriminate between the sane and the Nancy?

Not that I could even surmise what it is that Ted Nancy is actually after. He certainly doesn't seem to want any of these things—for which he so passionately strives—for very long. He seems to inexplicably flit from one thing to another like a monkey on a fast-food griddle:

"I look like Chester A. Arthur and I want to go to a football game."

"I'm painted orange and I need to stay in your hotel."

"I love your fork!"

What is his compulsion to disturb innocent, honest, hardworking people? People who are doing nothing more than attempting to conduct their daily business in a dignified fashion.

Why write to a wedding chapel in Las Vegas requesting to have sex in their office after the ceremony? And then when they refuse, to not take no for an answer. To write back again and again. "We would really like to have sex in your office." Does anyone deserve to be accosted in this way?

What is even the entertainment value in reading these imbecilic missives? Don't we want people doing their jobs and contributing to the growth of our nation? Or do we want them sidetracked for hours by this addle-brained, one-man Special Olympics? Do the good civil servants of Las Cruces, New Mexico, really need to step away from their desks to respond to a sub-moronic concept like selling fried chum to the general public through a chain of 1,032 Hungry Mosquito-themed restaurants all supposedly opening on the same day? Does a plastic surgeon need to take time out of his day to deal with a request to have a big toe grafted onto someone's face where his nose used to be? I think perhaps not.

I used to wonder if someday I would even find the real Ted L. Nancy. Now I worry that he someday will find me.

—Jerry Seinfeld
February 1998

MORE Letters
from a Nut

WHAT'S KOOKIN'?

560 No. Moorpark Rd. #236
Thousand Oaks, CA 91360

Aug 27, 1996

Customer Service Dept.
GOOD COOK DINNER FORK CO.
BRADSHAW INTERNATIONAL, INC
9303 Greenleaf Ave
Santa Fe Springs, CA 90670

Dear Customer Service Dept.,

I just want to tell you how happy I am with my fork. I use it all
the time. In this world of people not giving others credit I just
want to say that the Good Cook Dinner Fork company makes a very
good fork. Maybe the best fork I have ever used! Certainly
better than my spoon.

I use your fork on the following: mashed potatoes, melon chunks,
cranberry roll, beets, corn, lettuce, cake.

Please let me know that the people who made my fork were thanked.
They deserve more than just looking at forks all day. Let them
know others are out there and they care!!! Thank you.

I look forward to hearing from you soon. In the meantime I will
continue to use my fork on the following: Sandwich meat, pie,
pineapple, imitation crab, yams, rice, gumbo.

Will you be coming out with any new fork designs soon? I like my
fork, but I want to be up to date on other fork designs. Will
there be more prongs? I am satisfied with the number of prongs I
have now, but you never know. Thanks for thanking the fork makers
for me and writing me back and telling me they were thanked.
Thanks.

Best Wishes,

Ted L. Nancy

Ted L. Nancy

Bradshaw International, Inc.

August 28, 1996
BB-1429

Mr. Ted L. Nancy
560 No. Moorpark Road, #236
Thousand Oaks, CA 91360

Dear Mr. Nancy,

We received your letter and are very happy you like your fork.

I assure you, we will thank the manufacturers of the fork.

We are always developing new products, so keep your eyes peeled and watch for a new fork!

Sincerely,
BRADSHAW INTERNATIONAL, INC.

Brett Bradshaw
Brand Manager

BB:kmb

9303 Greenleaf Avenue
Santa Fe Springs, CA 90670
(310) 946-7466
FAX (310) 946-6070
(800) 421-6290

560 No. Moorpark Rd. #236
Thousand Oaks, CA 91360

Oct 25, 1996

Administration
THE COCA COLA COMPANY
1 Coca Cola Plz., NW
Atlanta, GA 30313

Dear Coca Cola:

I have a beverage called Kiet Doke. Will it interfere with your
beverage - Diet Coke. The taste is NOT SIMILAR at all!! (Mine
tastes like Pepsi).

I sell my Kiet Doke to mostly construction workers who love it.
One guy said, "This sure DOESN'T taste like Coca Cola."

Let me know so I can continue to sell my soda. Thanks. By the
way do you use caramel in your soda? Just checking. Thanks.

Sincerely,

Ted L. Nancy

Ted L. Nancy

The Coca-Cola Company

COCA-COLA PLAZA
ATLANTA, GEORGIA

LEGAL DIVISION

January 9, 1997

ADDRESS REPLY TO
P.O. DRAWER 1734
ATLANTA, GA 30301

404 676-2121
OUR REFERENCE NO.

Mr. Ted L. Nancy
560 No. Moorpark Road #236
Thousand Oaks, CA 91360

       RE: KIET DOKE (Our Reference Number 145342)

Dear Mr. Nancy:

     Thank you for your letter of October 25, 1996 inquiring whether you may continue using the trademark KIET DOKE in association with a beverage.

     As the owner of a federal registration for the famous trademark "diet Coke", we cannot consent to your use of KIET DOKE in association with a beverage. We believe KIET DOKE is confusingly similar to our trademark "diet Coke", and are concerned that an appreciable number of consumers will believe that The Coca-Cola Company endorses your product. As a result, we must insist that you immediately take action to discontinue use of KIET DOKE.

     If you are willing to immediately cease and desist using KIET DOKE, and agree not to use any product name or trademark similar to trademarks of The Coca-Cola Company in association with beverages in the future, please sign the spaces provided and return this letter to me. If you would like to discuss this, I may be reached at the numbers below. If we have not received this signed agreement within fifteen (15) days of the date of this letter, we will assume you do not agree to these terms.

              Sincerely,

              Nancy V. Stephens
              Trademark Counsel
              (404) 676-3035-Telephone - (404) 676-7682-Fax

Acknowledged and agreed to
this ___ day of _____, 1997
on behalf of _____

_____
SIGNATURE OF OFFICER

_____

560 No Moorpark Rd. #236
Thousand Oaks, CA 91360

Mar 29, 1997

MS. NANCY V. STEPHENS
COCA COLA
PO Drawer 1734
Atlanta, GA 30301

Dear Ms. Nancy V. Stephens,

I have decided that I will <u>not</u> sell my KIET DOKE beverage any
more. The product is discontinued. I am taking my $700.00 out of
the bank and my 11 cans of Kiet Doke that are left and bringing
them home. (They are in my room now).

I now realize it was a poorly thought out idea. It was stupid. I
mean if you went to 7-11 and saw in the cooler Dr. Pepper, Orange
Crush, Wink, and Kiet Doke would you choose Kiet Doke? I don't
think so. The idea was bad. Who was I to think that someone
would choose Kiet Doke? I am embarrassed over what I now consider
to be a terrible idea.

So let this letter stand as my admission that I have ceased and
desisted. There will be no more Kiet Doke on the market. I am
sorry I bothered you. I am sorry I wasted your time.

And please look out for my new beverage - PIET DEPSI. With the
familiar slogan: "It Tastes Nothing Like Coke!" (Will be in
coolers soon). Piet Depsi is a thirst quenching drink which, I
believe, does not taste like your drink.

Enjoy it! Also, what about the caramel in your soda? Are you
using a lot of it? Thanks.

Respectfully,

Ted L. Nancy

Ted L. Nancy

Dining Room Reservations
SUTTON PLACE HOTEL
4500 MacArthur Blvd.
Newport Beach, CA 92660   Sep 4, 1996

Dear Reservations Booker,

I belong to a Male Tickle Club. We want to hold our Tickle
Meeting at your restaurant. There are approximately 51 males who
are ticklish. We come in 16 cars. We DO NOT engage in any
tickling of each other at these meetings!

We gather once a month at various restaurants to hold our
meetings. I am in charge of finding the place that best
accommodates our needs. There is NO tickling at these gatherings.
Just _discussion_ about tickling. (Fingers, feathers, paper, light
bamboo, etc.). If someone is caught tickling, they are dismissed.
You will NOT be subjected to any behavior where there is tickling
going on. These rules are strictly enforced. NO TICKLING!

We need the following:

125 pounds of shrimp
116 garlic rolls
22 paper tickle aprons (Only officers and guests get aprons)

Can you give me a figure or let me know who I talk to to discuss
this?

We want to hold our next meeting at the end of September. This is
the best tickle weather. Please write with information so we can
proceed. Thank you. Again, these are only discussions and
lectures regarding tickling. There is no tickling activity.

Sincerely,

Ted L. Nancy
Good Tickling

Sept 1 1996

Dear Mr Nancy

Thank you for your interest in our restaurant.

The items needed for your event beeing somewhat different than what we usually serve, I would need some more specifics as too the type of food, the preparation, the set up the time and date.

Please feel free to contact me at your earliest convenience with all the informations that you might have for me—

Sincerely.

Dominique Roche
Accents Manager

At The Sutton Place Hotel

4500 MacArthur Boulevard • Newport Beach, California • 92660 • Tel: (714) 476-2001

560 No. Moorpark Rd. Apt. #236
Thousand Oaks, California 91360 USA

HIS ROYAL HIGHNESS PRINCE PHILIP MOUNTBATTEN
Duke Of Edinburgh
Buckingham Palace
London SW1 England   Mar 17, 1997

Dear HRH Prince Philip,

I want to take the time to tell you that I think the people of
England are a great bunch of persons. I have always admired
certain things the English people contribute but I think the
greatest is your lunch menu. Certainly the British noodle dish is
the finest dish out there. I eat it all the time. I serve it to
others, I tell people about it, I talk it up. I am 100 percent
behind these noodles!

Where did you come up with this combination? Chicken, soft
noodles, lettuce, pepper, vinaigrette, croutons, peanuts? It's
all there. You can't ask for anything more from a noodle dish.

You can tell your people that they can be proud because Americans
are eating their delicious food, not only as an appetizer but as a
main lunch meal! How about that? Is there any way to get the
perfect British noodle recipe from you? I will treasure it
forever knowing it came from a man with your dignity. I am truly
impressed with your Royal status and, of course, your noodles.

Will you write me and let me know that you got my letter? It
would be an honor to have a letter from the Duke Of Edinburgh, the
place where I get my noodles. You are the leader of the greatest
people in the world! May you be Duke forever; may you make this
dish forever. God bless you, Prince Philip! Will you send me an
autograph?

Respectfully,

Ted L. Nancy

Ted L. Nancy
Please send me a picture of you for my buffet.

From: Captain the Hon. James Geddes, GREN GDS

BUCKINGHAM PALACE

2nd April 1997

Dear Mr Nancy.

The Duke of Edinburgh has asked me to
thank you for your letter, the contents of which have
been noted.

Yours Sincerely

James Geddes

Temporary Equerry

Mr Ted Nancy

BY AIR MAIL
par avion
Rest of Mail

Mr Ted Nancy,
560 Moorpark Road,
Apt. #236,
Thousand Oaks,
California 91360,
USA.

560 No. Moorpark Rd. #236
Thousand Oaks, CA 91360

Nov 3, 1997

Mail Box Rentals
DENTON MAIN POST OFFICE
101 E McKinney St.
Denton, TX 76201

Dear Post Office,

I will be traveling to Denton and staying for 3,922 days. Every
day I will have a stuffed potato sent to me. Early in the week I
will have a bacon and cheese stuffed potato sent to me. Then
later in the week I will have a guacamole stuffed potato sent.
Some of these potatoes may smell. Especially if I don't pick up
my mail for a few months. I will deodorize the box.

I look forward to renting a post office box from you. Do you have
refrigerated post office boxes? Please let me know what I need
to rent this box for the duration of my stay.

Sincerely,

Ted L. Nancy

Ted L. Nancy

UNITED STATES
POSTAL SERVICE

November 18, 1997

Ted L Nancy
560 N Moorpark Rd #236
Thousand Oaks CA 91360

Dear Mr. Nancy:

This is in response to your recent letter concerning a post office box rental.

Enclosed please find PS Form 1093, Application for Post Office Box or Caller Service to be completed and returned to our office. The box rent fee is $20.00 for six (6) months or $40.00 for one (1) year.

If you have any questions or need further information, please contact our office at (940) 387-8555.

Sincerely,

Buck Ray
Officer-In-Charge
U. S. Postal Service
101 E. McKinney St
Denton, TX 76201-9998

:hm

enclosure

Reservations
L'ORANGERIE RESTAURANT
903 N. La Cienega Blvd.
Hollywood, CA 90069   Aug 27, 1996

Dear Reservations:

I wish to dine in your restaurant on the evening of Sunday, Sept
29, 1996. I have a situation which I must address.

I travel with my own waiter. I have found this waiter to be the
best for me in serving me my food. He has been with me for many
years. He brings me my soup hot and my salad with just the right
amount of dressing. (Vinaigrette).

My waiter will not interfere with your staff. He will work with
them to give me the best service available. I will leave my
waiter a gratuity.

I have heard L'Orangerie goes out of it's way for it's diners.
Especially those that bring their own waiter.

My party will be a large one and having my own waiter will insure
that service is impeccable. Please contact me so that we may make
arrangements for the Sept 29, 1996 dinner. Thank you very much.
I look forward to hearing from you soon.

Sincerely,

Ted L. Nancy

September 17, 1996

Mr. Ted Nancy
560 North Moorpark Road, #236
Thousand Oaks, CA 91360

Dear Mr. Nancy:

We are in receipt of your letter regarding a reservation at L'Orangerie and also requesting to bring your own waiter.

We need more information about the reservation and would appreciate if you could call me personally so we could do the necessary arrangements and requests for your party.

I am always at the restaurant anytime from 2:00 p.m. You could also leave any message to my secretary, Josephine.

Thank you.

Sincerely,

Christian Vanneque
General Manager

RELAIS &
CHATEAUX

903 North La Cienega Boulevard • Los Angeles, California 90069 • (310) 652-9770 • FAX 310-652-8870

560 No. Moorpark Rd.
Apt # 236
Thousand Oaks, CA 91360

Aug 22, 1996

Customer Service Dept.
MOTHER'S CAKE & COOKIE COMPANY
810 81st Ave
Oakland, CA 94621

Dear Mother's Cookie Co.,

I heard that you were coming out with the soft chip. I like the
soft cookie but don't you think the soft chip will be hard to eat?
It's not even a chip anymore. Instead of altering an old snack
why don't you get a "brand new" snack? You could call it "The
Slappy."

The real problem with the soft chip is it will become soggy and
bend. It will not stay up! Hard chips can be grabbed by the
teeth before the fingers reach lips. You can't dip the soft chip.
You might as well put dip on your fingers and lick it off.

I thought you guys do research and development on these things.
Has no one brought up the problems you will have with the soft
chip? Any openings in Research and Development? I have some
great new chip ideas.

How about a semi hard, chewy chip you can re-dip? It would come
with a personal dip cup for sanitation purposes. I look forward
to hearing from you regarding "The Slappy."

Sincerely,

Ted L. Nancy

August 27, 1996

Mr. Ted L. Nancy
560 No. Moorpark Rd., Apt. 236
Thousand Oaks, CA 91360

Dear Mr. Nancy:

Thank you for your recent letter concerning Mother's
products which are available. Since it is our
objective to produce items ur consumers want, we are
always interested in hearing comments firsthand.

Your suggestion for "The Slappy" chip will be passed
along to our product development department, who are
constantly working on new items.

The soft chip you mentioned you heard we were coming
out with is news to us. A soft chip would be, as you
mentioned, very impractical and is not anything we are
considering.

We appreciate your interest in our products and hope
you will feel free to write whenever you have a
question or comment.

Have a good day.

Sincerely,

Jackie Dalke

Jacqueline Dalke
Consumer Services Manager

Encl.

Mother's Cake & Cookie Co. • 810-81st Avenue • Oakland, CA 94621-2583 • (510) 569-2323 • FAX (510) 569-6604

560 No. Moorpark Rd. #236
Thousand Oaks, CA 91360

Nov 20, 1996

Customer Service
HILSHIRE FARMS
P.O. Box 227
New London, WI 54961

Dear Hilshire Farms,

I understand you make boneless frog nuts. I think this is the
perfect bar snack. Better than cashews. While in New Zealand I
ate them all the time and I don't like frog!

Please send me your complete line of boneless frog nuts gift tins.
Thank you. Good to see them here in America.

Sincerely,

Ted L. Nancy

Hillshire Farm & Kahn's

Division of Sara Lee Corporation

December 2, 1996

Mr. Ted L. Nancy
560 No. Moorpack Rd #236
Thousand Oaks, CA 91360

Dear Mr. Nancy:

Thank you for inquiring about the availability of a boneless frog
nut product.

We regret to inform you that Hillshire Farm does not produce such
a product. We hope you will continue to look for our fine
quality products in your local retail market.

Enclosed are complimentary product coupons which we hope you will
use toward future Hillshire Farm and Kahn's purchases. Also
enclosed are recipes we hope you will enjoy using to discover
some of the many ways our smoked sausage products can be prepared
and enjoyed.

Cordially Yours,

Vickie Moffitt

Vickie Moffitt
Consumer Affairs Representative

                        ENCLOSURES: RB001 SC016
                                    HAMBR EN001
                                    LC001
                                    SC015

560 No. Moorpark Rd #236
Thousand Oaks, CA 91360

Sep 30, 1996

Reservations
THE RITZ CARLTON, BUCKHEAD
3434 Peachtree Rd. NE
Atlanta, GA 30326

Dear Ritz Carlton Reservations Desk,

I would like to check into your resort for a week starting
October 30th. I have a problem which I like to address to hotels
when traveling. I eat my bedding. I chew my mattress, I eat my
pillows. Can you give me a flat rate so that I will not be
charged an excessive amount for the bedding I chew and nibble on?
Or should I bring my own bedding?   I have heard that the Ritz
Carlton goes out of its way for its guests. I am sorry that I eat
through my mattress. This is something I have to deal with.
Believe me it's tough. I have to travel though. That's why I
would like a set fee on what my charge would be for the room, and
for the chewed and partially eaten bedding. Please take a credit
card imprint from me when I check in.

If the Oct 30th start date is unavailable, can you offer me
another date? I really like your hotel and I want to be honest
with you regarding my dilemma. Thank you very much for your
response. I would like to make reservations as soon as possible,
(If I can), as I am making my travel schedule now. Thanks.

Sincerely,

Ted L. Nancy

THE RITZ-CARLTON ®
BUCKHEAD

February 17, 1997

Mr. Ted L. Nancy
560 North Moorpark Road
#236
Thousand Oaks CA 91360

Dear Mr. Nancy,

Thank you for your request for room availability. The rate I would have available for March 9-15, 1997, is $250.00 per evening for an Executive Suite.

Please advise if you would like to book your reservation. We can also be reached by phone (404)237-2700 or facsimile (404)240-7191. Again, thank you for your interest in The Ritz-Carlton, Buckhead.

Sincerely,

Christie Cammack
Room Reservations

560 No. Moorpark Rd #236
Thousand Oaks, CA 91360

Aug 1, 1996

SARA LEE CAKES
224 South Michigan
Chicago, Illinois 60604

Dear Sara Lee,

I want to tell you an incident that happened to me yesterday. I
have enjoyed your cookies, cakes, and goodies for years. I weigh
quite a bit from eating Sara Lee. (500). I know your slogan is
"NOBODY DOESN'T LIKE SARA LEE."

Yesterday at my mosh party I put out one of your fudgie swirl
cakes. A female guest (also heavy - 600) said to me "I don't like
this." I said, "What do you mean? Nobody doesn't like Sara Lee."
She said, "Well, I don't like it."

One thing led to another and she came at me with a shrimp fork.
(She punctured my arm. Didn't break skin - luckily).

My question: She accused me of using poor English by saying
Nobody doesn't like Sara Lee. Is this poor English? Who is using
poor English?   You and me or her?   Can you tell me?

Also, can you give me a list of your cakes that I can send her so
she will find A SNACK SHE LIKES. To me, everybody do not like
something, but NOBODY can say they will do not like Sara Lee.

Thank you for clearing this English thing up.

Sincerely,

Ted L. Nancy

August 14, 1996

Mr. Ted Nancy
560 N. Moorpark Road #236
Thousand Oaks, CA 91360

Dear Mr. Nancy:

Thank you for taking the time to contact Sara Lee Bakery. Your comments
will be passed to the many people involved in developing, producing, and
marketing our baked goods.

The slogan has been "Nobody Doesn't Like Sara Lee" since 1968. It was
just a catchy phrase that stuck with us. It is meant for product
recognition, not as a teaching tool. We apologize for any confusion this
has caused.

We would like to show our appreciation for your time. Enclosed are
coupons for you to use on your next shopping trip.

Sincerely,

Tracie McCarthy
Consumer Services

0103818A

THE HUNGRY MOSQUITO
Family Restaurants
Ted L. Nancy, President

Ted L. Nancy
560 No. Moorpark Rd. #236
Thousand Oaks, CA 91360

Business Registrations Dept.
CITY OF LAS CRUCES
251 W Amador Ave. #103
Las Cruces, NM 88005-2800   Apr 15, 1997

Dear Business Registrations Dept:

I wish to get a Business Registration to open my HUNGRY MOSQUITO
restaurants in your city. The Hungry Mosquito is a family dining
restaurant specializing in fried chum.

Our logo is a 10 foot high sign of a human forearm with a mosquito
biting it. (There will be some blood).

There will be 1,032 restaurants in Las Cruces all opening on the
same day. (Four in the mall). At its height there will be 52,000
people in mosquito outfits walking the streets, riding the buses,
dating your women. The outfit is: A mosquito body with spindly
legs, big eyes, a stinger.

Please tell me how I get a permit to operate my 1,032 HUNGRY
MOSQUITO restaurants in Las Cruces? I have always admired the way
you feed people in your city. I believe you have a Shoneys there.

Thank you very much in writing me with information on permits.
And please, stop by for a complimentary dish of chum in any of the
1,032 Hungry Mosquito restaurants - Las Cruces' place for bucket
fish.

Sincerely,

Ted L. Nancy
Ted L. Nancy

 City of Las Cruces

April 30, 1997

Mr. Ted L. Nancy
560 No. Moorpark Rd. #236
Thousand Oaks, CA 91360

Dear Mr. Nancy:

Thank you for your inquiry on obtaining 1,032 Hungry Mosquito Restaurants in Las Cruces. I have discussed your proposal with the appropriate staff, and I believe there may be some problems which you have not anticipated.

    1. *Sign*: Your human forearm with a mosquito biting it can be permitted for the appropriate fee and if all setbacks and traffic applications are met. However, we cannot approve the use of blood unless it has been previously approved in writing by the Board of Directors of the Environmental Improvement Division, the Regional Headquarters of the American Red Cross, and our internal Risk Management Department Director (to ensure no contamination could possibly occur to restaurant-goers). We would seriously encourage you to utilize a recycled paint, provided it does not violate the lead content or our Household Hazardous Wastes Ordinance. You will have to obtain the approval of the Director of the State Environmental Improvement Division, and the Federal Environmental Department, and our Director of Utilities Division (to ensure no contamination could possibly occur to our groundwater strata or the nearby Rio Grande River). Depending upon the analysis of the material utilized, it may also be necessary for you to obtain permission from the International Boundary Water Commission, the Texas Department of Water Ways, and the Mexican Government (to ensure no contamination could possibly occur to residents downstream of the river).

P.O. DRAWER CLC
LAS CRUCES, NEW MEXICO 88004
(505) 526-0000

AN EQUAL OPPORTUNITY EMPLOYER
Recycled Paper

2.   ***Mosquito Outfits***:   You will be required to obtain the appropriate approvals from the United States Wearing Apparel Unions and the United Workers of America to utilize the proposed mosquito outfits.   Under no circumstances may the City of Las Cruces Business Registrations Department grant you permission to copy, imitate or suggest an imitation of any previously patented or copyrighted design. Additionally, because of our intense sun during the summer months, you will be required to obtain permission from the Environmental Department for the textiles utilized in the fabrication of the outfit to ensure there is no potential for temperature extremes through the fabric to the wearer.   Our internal Risk Manager has also indicated that he will require individually signed waivers from all persons wearing these outfits, along with affidavits from their personal physicians that there is no potential for health related problems due to the sun damage to materials in this environment.

One related problem that may arise concerning the outfits is the utilization of our transit system. Riders of the system are required to ensure that they have no luggage, baggage or other materials that might restrict or hinder the free passage of the bus aisle by other riders. Any individual wearing a mosquito outfit that allows the spindly legs or stinger to violate this rule will be immediately evicted from the bus, despite the present location of the bus. This could pose a safety problem to other pedestrians or drivers utilizing the roadways during heavy vehicular traffic times at overpasses and busy intersections. Therefore, all riders in mosquito outfits will be required to remove their outfits prior to boarding the bus. Please note, we do have anti-nudity laws in Las Cruces, and the Police Department has been advised to watch for individuals stripping from mosquito outfits and then boarding the transit buses to ensure all necessary portions of the body are appropriately covered during the process.

Another problem that could possibly occur because of the proposed outfits is your mention of people in mosquito outfits dating our women. We understand that California does have other standards from the rest of the country. However, in New Mexico we do not approve of women trying to pick up other women, regardless of whether the picker upper is dressed in a mosquito outfit or not (We do have approved sites for this type of behavior, should your employees be interested). You must warn the individuals utilizing the outfits that they could be putting themselves in danger from outraged females or from undercover cops posing as "Mosquito Molls" to entrap these individuals.

     3.   **_Permitting_**: Permitting of your 1,032 Hungry Mosquito Restaurants is possibly one of the more time consuming processes of opening an enterprise of this size in Las Cruces. Each individual site must meet the appropriate zoning, overlay design and traffic standards criteria, and if necessary obtain the appropriate residential neighborhood association approval. Each permit cost will vary according to how much we believe we can get from you, with the cost escalating for each permit as it is obtained. We do not permit certain color schemes in certain areas (such as the historic districts), and you will be required to obtain the appropriate board/committee approval and pay for those appropriate reviews prior to obtaining the permit. You must, of course, obtain the approval of the United States Environmental Department, the New Mexico Environmental Department, the New Mexico Association of Respected Restaurateurs, and the Las Cruces Business Advisory Group prior to receiving final approval to open your restaurants. Your fees for any previous approvals are non-refundable should you not obtain the latter approvals.

     I have enclosed the appropriate preliminary application. Please make the appropriate copies and return them with your initial, non-refundable fee of $1,500 each, to my office. Thank you for your interest in opening your businesses in Las Cruces. We are always interested in improving our economic development through the establishment of profitable enterprises.

Mr. Nancy
April 30, 1997
Page 4

On behalf of all Las Cruces, thank you for your correspondence.   We
definitely believe your proposal sucks.

Sincerely,

Debbie T. Calderon
Business Permits Review
P.O. Box 20000
Las Cruces, NM 88004

Enclosure - 1

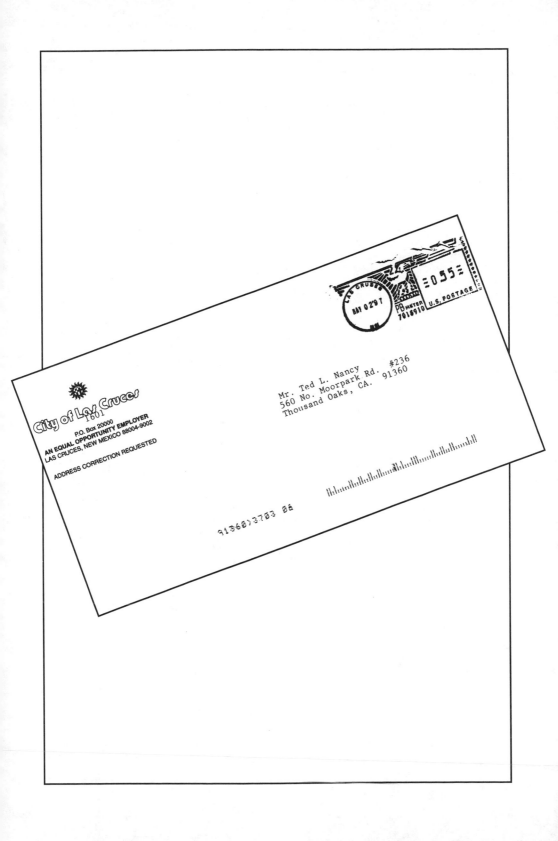

City of Las Cruces
1601
P.O. Box 20000
AN EQUAL OPPORTUNITY EMPLOYER
LAS CRUCES, NEW MEXICO 88004-9002

ADDRESS CORRECTION REQUESTED

LAS CRUCES
MAY 02 97
NM

PB METER
7018910   U.S. POSTAGE   ≡05.5≡

Mr. Ted L. Nancy   #236
560 No. Moorpark Rd.   91360
Thousand Oaks, CA.

91360)3783 05

i'm
OUT WITH PEOPLE

560 North Moorpark Road #236
Thousand Oaks, California 91360

Reservations
RHETT HOUSE HOTEL
1009 Craven St.
Beaufort, SC 29902   Aug 27, 1996

Dear Reservation Desk:

I wish to check into your fine hotel on September 29, 1996 for one
evening. I wish to stay in a suite. My problem:

I have an aversion to all germs. Therefore I travel with my own
toilet seat and portable shower. I wear a body sheath when I
sleep in a strange room. Can I be accomodated?

I will put down a protective splash when eating at your buffet.
This protective splash will cover me and the area directly around
me. It is similar to a tent, but I can see through it. Will it
interfere with other diners?

I believe I will catch the diseases of others if I do not protect
myself. I wear a dribble poncho and use calf lining for my feet
when I walk across the room. My hands are covered in knuckle gum.

I put a cellophane area around the toilet then put down my own
toilet seat. I use cardboard over my head then sit down and
relieve myself. This is the only way I cam be sure that the
diseases of others will not get me.

Please give me your best corporate rate for that evening and let
me know that my special cleanliness equipment will be allowed in
your hotel.

I have often heard that the Rhett House hotel allows it's guest
specialties to accommodate them. Thank you. I look forward to
hearing from you soon regarding my September 29, 1996 stay

Sincerely,

Ted L. Nancy

The Rhett House INN

September 6, 1996

Mr. Ted L. Nancy
560 North Moorpark Road #236
Thousand Oaks, CA 91360

Mr. Nancy:

We received your letter dated August 27, regarding the possibility of reserving a room on September 29. We do have rooms available for that evening, although we do not have any suites in the inn. Your best bet would be room 10, which is our deluxe room with a king sized bed, a private entrance and screened verandah, and a jacuzzi.

We would be glad to accommodate you and your special equipment for the evening. I do not anticipate that your provisions will pose a problem to the inn or our other guests. However, none of us is sure what knuckle gum is and our only concern would be if it would stain the linens or bedding.

Feel free to call us at (803) 524-9030 for further information about our inn, and to discuss a reservation for the evening of September 29. We look forward to hearing from you!

Sincerely,

Molly Wilson
Innkeeper

560 North Moorpark Road
#236
Thousand Oaks, CA 91360

Sep 9, 1996

Reservations
HYATT REGENCY SAN DIEGO
1 Market Pl.
San Diego, CA 92101

Dear Reservations,

I will need a room for one night, Oct 12, 1996. I have a
sickness.

I am a kleptomaniac. I will steal your lamps, mattress, clock
radio, even the ice machine from the hallway vending area. I want
to tell you about this before I check in so that when you see the
room completely empty after I leave you will understand.

Naturally, I will compensate you for whatever I take.

Can the staff be notified when they see me trying to put a
mattress in my car and drive away?   Can they be made aware that a
kleptomaniac is staying at the hotel?

I will take your sheets, pillowcase, comforter off the bed, and
try and get your dresser out of the room. When I get home and
realize what I have done I will call you and we can arrange for
you to come and get your furniture. (I hope I give you the
correct dresser). For your protection, please inventory the room
and get a credit card imprint from me.

Is the Oct 12th date available? Please write and let me know.
Thank you. I look forward to a pleasant stay with you on that
evening.

Sincerely,

Ted L. Nancy

Hyatt Regency San Diego
On San Diego Bay
One Market Place
San Diego, CA 92101 USA

Telephone: 619.232.1234
FAX: 619.239.5678

September 30, 1996

Ted L. Nancy
560 North Moorpark Road
#236
Thousand Oaks, CA 91360

Dear Mr. Nancy,

Thank you for your letter dated September 9th, 1996 requesting reservations at our hotel. Due to the content of the letter we are unable to offer you accommodations.

Sincerely,

Gordon G. Redding
Director of Security

560 North Moorpark Road
#236
Thousand Oaks, California
91360

SEABOURN CRUISE LINES
55 Francisco St
San Francisco, CA 94133   1 Aug 1996

Dear Cruise Booker,

My friend and I would like to book passage on your magnificent sea
voyage. I have a situation which I need to address.

My friend has been diagnosed with multiple personalities. He has
9 distinct personalities. But let me tell you, he's a great bunch
of guys. His name is Frito

In a controlled atmosphere he is okay. It's when he gets back to
the room that's when he sometimes gets belligerent and I have some
trouble with him and he may need supervision.

Frito has been my companion forever. I don't go anywhere without
him. We have traveled extensively throughout the Pacific Rim. He
is a sensitive, caring individual but he has 9 personalities.
Sometimes he is angry, sometimes sad. Sometimes he blushes,
sometimes he is very argumentative. But that is the way Frito is.
What can I do?

Can I get a reservation for the two (9) of us? Do we need that
many rooms? How many stewards can we be assigned? Let us know
the cost. We want to sail the week of September 15th, 1996 when
the waters are ice cold.

Please write and let me know if Frito and me are accepted on your
sea vessel. Thank you for understanding our needs. I will show
up by myself the day of the cruise then Frito will come later.

Sincerely,

Ted L. Nancy

(Frito hates limes!)

SEABOURN
CRUISE LINE

November 27, 1996

Ted L. Nancy
560 N Moorpark Rd # 236
Thousand Oaks CA 91360-3703

An Invitation to Seabourn Club Membership

Dear Ted L. Nancy,

I am writing to invite you to sail with Seabourn Cruise Line and join the most exclusive group of international travelers in the world, the *Seabourn Club*.

The Seabourn Club is distinguished by its members—the Seabourn guests who have sailed our world since we began cruising in 1988. We are proud of our guests. They bring a level of travel experience, worldliness and intellect we believe to be unrivaled by any other group of travelers. And we are honored that they trust Seabourn again and again to deliver the vacation experience and level of service that they recognize as uncompromising and unsurpassed.

But, Seabourn Club Membership carries a price; thus its exclusivity. As part of our 1997 membership drive, we are offering a one-time savings of $500 per person on a Seabourn 1997 vacation of choice* to vacationers that have not yet sailed with us, and hold no future reservation. This translates into $1,000 savings on a double occupancy suite.

After you have cruised with us once, you are a Seabourn Club Member and the benefits accumulate quickly. Members are entitled to an automatic 10% savings on designated Club sailings and friends that sail on the same voyage with a Club Member save 5%. What's more, once a Member has sailed 28 days with Seabourn, they are entitled to a 25% savings off of their next cruise. After 70 Days at Sea, a Member saves 50% on their next cruise, and after 140 Days at Sea, the subsequent 14 day sailing is complimentary, regardless of destination or published price. (There is never a "black-out" on Club Award sailings.) Members also receive the award-winning quarterly magazine, *Seabourn Club Herald*, reduced travel insurance, and recognition gifts and parties.

Enclosed is a brochure to give you a taste of the Seabourn experience and a Membership Savings Invitation. We look forward to welcoming you aboard and into the Seabourn Club.

Sincerely,

Larry Pimentel

Larry Pimentel
President

P.S. This is a limited one-time offer only valid on a new reservation made and deposited between November 30, 1996 and January 31, 1997 by a non-Club Member. You must present the enclosed invitation to your travel agent or Seabourn to receive the savings. *The 1997 voyage must be 5 or more days in length. A handful of dates are blacked out due to being already sold-out or holiday departures, but good space still exists on most other sailings.

55 FRANCISCO STREET, SAN FRANCISCO, CALIFORNIA 94133
PHONE: (415) 391-7444 • TELEFAX: (415) 391-8518
TELEX: 205838 SEBRN UR

560 No. Moorpark Rd. #236
Thousand Oaks, CA 91360

Sep 23, 1996

Customer Service
HOLLAND AMERICA CRUISE LINE
300 Elliot Ave. W.
Seattle, WA 98119

Dear Customer Service:

I want to take a cruise the last week of October, 1996. I have a
predicament which I want to bring to your attention.

I have a permanent squeak when I walk. At first I thought it was
my shoes but I took them off and the squeak persisted. Then I
took off all my clothes (except underwear) and the squeak was
still there. Finally I was stark naked and I took a few steps and
I still heard the squeak. What can I do? I have to walk

Can I get passage on your cruise even with this permanent squeak?
It is very annoying I know but I want to enjoy your fine cruise.
I hope others will be tolerant of me when they hear me walk by.

Please let me know if you have space available for me to cruise at
the end of October and if my squeak will be permitted on board.
Thank you very much. I look forward to hearing from you soon as I
want to make my reservation now.

Respectfully,

Ted L. Nancy

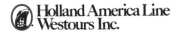

Holland America Line
Westours Inc.

October 2, 1996

Mr. Ted L. Nancy
560 North Moorpark Road #236
Thousand Oaks, CA 91360

Dear Mr. Nancy,

Thank you for your September 23 letter. We are very glad you are considering a cruise with Holland America Line.

Please be assured we have many physically challenged passengers aboard our cruise ships. Many passengers travel in wheelchairs, use crutches, require full time oxygen, dialysis or have various other ailments. You will not offend or bother anyone while aboard any of our cruise ships. Holland America Line encourages physically challenged passengers to travel with us by providing the best handicapped accommodations available in the industry.

We appreciate your taking the time to write to share your concerns. You may want to contact your travel planner soon if you are considering a cruise at the end of October. We look forward to the opportunity to serve you in the future. Thank you for considering Holland America Line and thank you for writing.

Sincerely,

Laurie Steele
Office of the Vice President
Reservations\Passenger Programs

300 Elliott Avenue West • Seattle, WA 98119 • 206 • 281-3535 • Fax: 206 • 281-7110

560 No. Moorpark Rd. #236
Thousand Oaks, CA 91360

Chief Of Security
Administration Dept.
NEW ORLEANS SAINTS FOOTBALL TEAM
901 Papworth Ave
Metairie, LA 70005   Sep 23, 1996

Dear Chief Of Security:

I will be arriving by rail, New Orleans, Louisiana, the last day
of September, 1996 for an extended stay. (2 years). I will be
visiting the Superdome for your sporting events on many occasions.
I have a situation which I must address:

I look just like Chester A. Arthur, our esteemed 21st president.
I am portly with mutton chop sideburns and a pressed waist coat.
I wear a size 52 slacks. My grayish hair is parted down the
middle. I have a walrus moustache. Naturally, I will need
special security when entering the Superdome so that others don't
accost me.

My safety is VERY important. As a look alike for Chester A.
Arthur, I have had things thrown at me and I have been cursed at
from others who don't believe in his policies. While I don't
agree with everything President Arthur said, he should be
respected. He had an honest, efficient, and dignified
administration. Do you have presidential boxes?

He was a collector of the port of New York before becoming
president. He became president after Garfield's assassination.
That is why I must have security. We don't need another blooper.
Can my safety be assured?   Please write and let me know so I can
make arrangements to see football. I am interested in season
tickets. Thanks.

Sincerely,

Ted L. Nancy
Chester A. Arthur

NEW ORLEANS LOUISIANA
SAINTS

Ted L. Nancy
560 No. Moorpark Rd. #236
Thousand Oaks, CA 91360

Dear Mr. Nancy,

I apologize for not writing back sooner. We have been very busy here in New Orleans. I have read your letters and considered them fully.

The Louisiana Superdome is a safe environment to watch a football game. The security is constantly upgraded and closely monitored. If, however, you would not feel comfortable sitting in the stands, we do have box suits available. I would be happy to discuss the possibility and availability of these suites with you.

I can also assure you that as a look alike for Chester A Aurthur you will not be frowned upon in the stadium. Down here in New Orleans we have become accustomed to the unusual and outlandish. At our last game for instance we had Don King, Elvis, and Abraham Lincoln look alikes all in the stands.

I hope this letter helps you out, but please feel free to call me at (504) 731-1789 if there is anything I can do to help. I hope your travels go well and if you do come to a game please call, because I would be interested in stopping by to meet a Chester A. Aurthur look alike myself.

Sincerely,

Grant Neill
New Orleans Saints Marketing

5800 Airline Highway • Metairie, LA 70003 • (504) 733-0255

ADMINISTRATION	MEDIA RELATIONS	PLAYER PERSONNEL	TICKET OFFICE
Fax (504) 731-1782	Fax (504) 731-1888	Fax (504) 731-1768	Fax (504) 731-1707

560 North Moorpark Road #236
Thousand Oaks, CA 91360

Sep 4, 1996

General Manager
LOEWS CORONADO BAY RESORT
4000 Coronado Bay Rd.
Coronado, CA 92118

Dear Hotel Manager:

I am interested in a suite at your hotel for the following dates:
Oct 3-Oct 4, 1996. This will be a business-personal trip. I have
a special request:

Although my name is Ted Nancy, I would like to be called Philippe
Spotto in the restaurant? I then would like to be called Fred
Chancy in the health club. While by your pool, I would like to be
addressed as Mr. Marco Salmon and then I want to be called Dr.
Frank Del Fudgio while in your lobby after checking in. I will
have different people with me when I arrive at these locations and
MUST be called these names for business purposes only.

I would like to be announced: "Mr. Fred Chancy and guest, we have
your treadmills ready." And, "Ah, it's Mr. Marco Salmon, welcome
to our cabana area and pool."

Perhaps a bellman could come up to me in the lobby and say, "Are
you Dr. Frank Del Fudgio? I have a message for you." Then
whisper in my ear, "It's just me."

Please let me know if I can be accomodated? And if the Oct 3-4
room is available? Thank you. I know the Coronado Bay Resort
goes out of it's way for it's travelers.

Sincerely,

Ted L, Nancy

LOEWS CORONADO BAY
R E S O R T

JOHN THACKER
REGIONAL VICE PRESIDENT
GENERAL MANAGER

September 9, 1996

Ted L. Nancy
560 North Moorpark Road, #236
Thousand Oaks, CA 91360

Dear Mr. Nancy:

Thank you for your interest in Loews Coronado Bay Resort. Unfortunately, we are sold out on October 3 and 4 and will not be able to honor your request. You may want to check with the Hotel del Coronado or Le Meridian in Coronado. Regarding your special requests, you may want to be more specific regarding which restaurant and how one will be able to recognize you at the particular locations.

Best of luck with your venture.

Sincerely,

John Thacker
General Manager

cc: Marco Salmon
       Fred Chancy
       Frank Del Fudgio
       Philippe Spotto

560 No. Moorpark Rd. #236
Thousand Oaks, CA 91360

Mar 31, 1997

MAYOR'S OFFICE, JACKSON
145 Broadway St.
Jackson, OH 45640-1656

Dear Mayor's Office,

I want to give back to the community. I want to stage the play
"Romeo and Juliet" using otter. There will be no racy scenes but
some holding. Otters will play Romeo, Juliet, and the others. We
will bring the otters out at intermission to pet. These otters
are something to see. They have performed this play many times
with only one biting incident.

I wish to put on a FREE performance in your downtown area for
workers. Or any other people the Mayor's Office deems necessary.
I want to give back to the community. Perhaps you have some folks
that could use a good otter rendition of this classic love story.
This is a sensitive, warm telling of the story using sea otters.
Audiences will like the otter grunts and sounds especially when
Romeo tells Juliet he loves her.

Ohio is the place. I have grand memories of the towns of this
great state.

Please let me know how I put on this free show for the good people
of Jackson? Thank you. Would you like to see a video tape of
the show? I look forward to hearing from you soon. All I
require are three stair ramps and a public address system.

Sincerely,

Ted L. Nancy

Honorable
John T. Evans
Mayor
(614) 286-3224

City of Jackson
Office of the Mayor

Memorial Building
145 Broadway
Jackson, Ohio
45640

April 15, 1997

Mr. Ted L. Nancy
560 No. Moorpark Rd. #236
Thousand Oaks, CA 91360

Dear Mr. Nancy:

Thank you for your letter of March 31, 1997, informing us that you would like to stage "Romeo and Juliet", in our area, using otter.

This sounds quite interesting; before we schedule a free show, we feel that we "otter" (no pun intended) view a video-tape of the show. Could you please send this to me; then, after reviewing the tape, I will contact you.

Again, thank you for your interest in our City; I look forward to receiving the video-tape.

Sincerely,

John T. Evans
Mayor
City of Jackson, Ohio

JTE/rrp

560 No. Moorpark Rd. Apt. #236
Thousand Oaks, CA 91360

City Events Department
City Hall
CITY OF BRADENTON
500 15th St. W
Bradenton FL 34205-6727   Feb 25, 1997

Dear City Events Office,

I understand the City of Bradenton will be sponsoring NUDE BALLOON
RACES this coming March 28th. What an event! I understand there
will be over 11,000 nude people converging on your beautiful city
racing each other with balloons tied to them. I can't wait!

Where can I sign up? I have long admired nude balloon races and
now I want to be a part of it. I have been involved in other nude
events. I was a nude traffic school instructor for the city of
Zarnsboro for 2 years.

I want to make one thing clear: This is not <u>nude hot air
balloning</u> where many naked people go up in a balloon. This is
nude people with balloons attached to them running down the
street.

Let me know where, when, and what about me?   Thank you. I look
forward to coming to your wonderful city and taking my clothes
off. Please write back with info on how I can do this. I need
lodging and food info. I look forward to hearing from you. Also,
will I need a sweater then? Is it cool?

Sincerely,

Ted L. Nancy

Ted L. Nancy

CITY OF BRADENTON
BRADENTON, FLORIDA

CARL CALLAHAN
CITY CLERK AND TREASURER

March 17th, 1997

Mr. Ted L. Nancy
560 N. Moorpark Rd.
#236
Thousand Oaks, CA 91360

Dear Mr. Nancy,

I received your letter of February 25th, 1997 regarding Nude Balloon Races in our City on March 28th, 1997.

To my knowledge there is no such event planned. The City has not received any application or requests for permits and I doubt very seriously the City Council would even approve it if the application was submitted.

However, thank you for your interest in our fine City, we have much to offer in other areas.

Sincerely,

Carl Callahan
City Clerk & Treasurer

560 No. Moorpark Rd. Apt. #236
Thousand Oaks, CA 91360

Mr. Carl Callahan
City Clerk & Treasurer
CITY OF BRADENTON
500 15th St. W
Bradenton, FL 34205-6727   Dec 15, 1997

Dear Mr. Callahan,

Thank very much for writing me back regarding the City Of
Bradenton's Nude Balloon Races. I am sorry to say I have been
misinformed. These are not <u>nude</u> <u>BALLOON</u> races. These are
<u>NUDE</u> <u>BABOON</u> races. I understand Bradenton will sponsor this for
January 28th, 1998.

Let me make one thing clear: These are not nude baboons racing
down the street. These are nude people with balloons attached to
them racing alongside baboons. There will be 11,000 nude <u>baboons</u>
racing down your streets. (And nude people)

Please send me information on: hotel, car rentals, baboon washes,
vaccines, clip-ons. It's nice that Bradenton thinks enough of its
citizens and guests to put on this much needed event. I commend
you! The one in France was a bust, so I hope this one goes
smoothly. Nude loose baboons can be dangerous. (Especially when
baboons AND people are nude). I have seen a biting incident.
That person was cited!

Thank you for answering my letter with city info.

Once again, I look forward to coming to Bradenton and taking off
my clothes.

Sincerely,

Ted L. Nancy
Ted L. Nancy

No Further Reply

CITY OF BRADENTON
CALLER SERVICE 25015
BRADENTON, FLORIDA 34206-5015

Mr. Ted L. Nancy
560 N. Moorpark Rd.
#236
Thousand Oaks, CA 91360

U.S. POSTAGE
0032

BRADENTON
JUL 18 '97
FL

560 No. Moorpark Rd. #236
Thousand Oaks, CA 91360

Sept 3, 1996

Tickets
SAN DIEGO PADRES
PO Box 2000
San Diego, CA 92112-2000

Dear Ticket Dept.,

I want to come and see the San Diego Padres play in September. I
love the Padres!   Go San Diego!

Because of my condition, I must walk with a portable shower over
my head. My entire head area is kept in a vinyl enclosure with a
shower constantly going on me. The top of my head must be kept
wet at all times!

While the top of my head needs to be soaked, my face and neck are
dry. They are kept dry with a portable dryer I have attached to
my collarbone. This dryer is similar to the one in a men's room.
While water drips on my face, a scoop under my neck drains the
water and it filters through my pants. The vinyl enclosure is
similar to a shower curtain. I can see the game this way.

Will this interfere with others? There is no wetness outside my
plastic casing. Thus, no one else will get sprinkled. Only the
top of my head will be drenched from my shower. I am sorry, but
this is because of my medical condition.

Please write and let me know if the portable shower over my head
will be okay for me to wear into the stadium. I may have to buy
the seat in back of me also. I need to know how much room between
rows. Thank you for your prompt reply as I MUST get my tickets
soon.

Respectfully,

Ted L. Nancy

Ted L. Nancy
Portable Shower Wearer #121

September 13, 1996

Mr. Ted L. Nancy
560 North Moorpark Road #236
Thousand Oaks, California 91360

Dear Mr. Nancy,

The Padres thank you for your letter of September 3. John Moores and Larry Lucchino are
committed to the fan, and they have done several things to prove this since purchasing the team
in 1994.

Please give me a call at 283-4494, extension 239, at your convenience. I would like to discuss
your letter further.

Thank you again for writing, and we hope that this response is timely.

Sincerely,

Mark Ferguson
Fan Services Representative

SAN DIEGO PADRES BASEBALL CLUB

P.O. BOX 2000, SAN DIEGO, CA 92112-2000 • 9449 FRIARS RD., SAN DIEGO, CA 92108-1771
TELEPHONE. 619 283 4494 • FAX: 619 292 2229

560 No. Moorpark Rd.
#236
Thousand Oaks, CA 91360

Feb 16, 1996

Reservations Desk
BEST WESTERN CONTINENTAL LODGE
1885 S. Virginia St
Reno, NV 89502

Dear Best Western Hotel Reservations:

I will be arriving by boat Mar 1, 1996 and wish to make
accomodations at your grand hotel for one night, Mar 10.

How can I be sure that I will be treated with utmost respect?   I
know your hotel prides itself on guest services. Can someone help
me with my needs when I check in? Can I get the proper respect
due me? I chose your hotel because of its dedication to its
guests. Others have told me of your devotion to service.

How can I be sure that I will get this service?   Can I be sure
that I will be given the proper respect?

Mar 10 is the date I like.   Can that be arranged? If not, can a
suitable date be arranged?   Do you offer this service?   Can I be
afforded the respect due me when I check in?   How will I know?
Who can assure me of this? Will I be respected?

Please advise me if that date is secure. Thank you very much.

Sincerely,

Ted L. Nancy

FEB. 26, 1996

DEAR MR. NANCY,

THANK YOU FOR YOUR INTEREST IN OUR HOTEL. I CAN ASSURE YOU THAT YOU WILL BE TREATED LIKE ALL OTHER PATRONS THAT STAY WITH US, AND THAT IS WITH RESPECT.

OUR STAFF IS READY TO HELP WITH YOUR NEEDS WHEN YOU CHECK IN, AS MUCH AS IS POSSIBLE.

AS OF THIS DATE WE DO HAVE AVAILABILITY ON MAR. 10. IF YOU WOULD LIKE A RESERVATION FOR THAT DATE, PLEASE CONTACT ME AND I WOULD BE MORE THAN HAPPY TO HELP YOU. OUR PHONE NUMBER IS 702-329-1001.

RESPECTFULLY

VINCENT CATAPANO

P.S. I HOPE YOU ARE AWARE WE DO NOT HAVE ANY DOCKING FACILITIES FOR YOUR BOAT.

THANK YOU ONCE AGAIN!!

i need more Help!

"THOSE STAINS ARE JUST HAIR DYE"
—PHYLLIS MURPHY

560 No. Moorpark RD #236
Thousand Oaks Calif 91360

Aug 1, 1996

Quality Control
BVD UNDERWEAR
PO Box 90015
Bowling Green, KY
42102-9015

Dear BVD Underwear:

I recently bought some of your underwear.

You say your leg openings stretch as you move. For me this is
wrong. When I move, my leg openings stay in the same place. Why?

Am I not moving my legs correctly? Please advise on how I should
move my legs. I have been moving my legs the same way for my
entire life. I don't want to move them differently now to
accommodate any underwear.

MY UNDERWEAR LEG OPENINGS ARE NOT STRETCHING!!   Perhaps I am
doing it wrong. I think you have the best underwear out there. I
wear a clean pair every day. Sometimes two a day If I have a
meeting. (Not at same time).

Thanks for getting back to me on this. I do not want to go back
to wearing ladies cotton underwear because their leg openings
stretch as I move.

What does BVD stand for? I have been trying to figure it out for
some time. Every once in a while I go back to it but I still
don't know. I can come up with the B and D but I never can figure
out the V.

Please, let everyone there know they make some good shorts. Could
be the best. Write me with leg opening info. Thanks.

Sincerely,

Ted L. Nancy

Fruit of the Loom, Inc.

FRUIT OF THE LOOM.

September 11, 1996

Mr. Ted L. Nancy
560 North Moorpark Road #236
Thousand Oaks, CA 91360

Dear Mr. Nancy:

Thank you for writing to Fruit of the Loom and BVD regarding our men's underwear. We are responding because we own both brands.

We were sorry to hear of the problem you have with the leg openings of the briefs
and apologize for your inconvenience. We haven't had any similar complaints and
without seeing the garments in question, we are unable to offer an explanation for
your experience.

If you will send the briefs to us, we will have our quality control department evalu-
ate the problem and follow-up with the factory. Of course, we will be happy to
replace or refund your money for them as well with postage costs included either
way (Parcel Post with minimum insurance or UPS).

We appreciate your cooperation, Mr. Nancy, and the time you took to write to us.

Sincerely,

Lynn Carter
Consumer Services

LC:lc

/si

P.S. By the way, BVD stands for Bradley, Voorhees and Day. These are the last
names of the three men who founded the company.

One Fruit of the Loom Drive
P.O. Box 90015
Bowling Green, KY 42102-9015   502-781-6400

560 North Moorpark Road
#236
Thousand Oaks, CA 91360

Sept 5, 1996

City Office
CITY OF OMAHA
1819 Farnam St.
Omaha, NE 68183

Dear City Office,

I am moving to Omaha soon and I am very concerned about your
traffic light system. I have heard that in early 1997 you will
change to the following traffic light system:

Red - Go
Green - Stop Suddenly
Yellow - Race Through Light
Plaid - Check Things Out, Then Proceed Accordingly

Why? I'm okay with everything but "Plaid." I think a plaid light
will be confusing for myself who has night vision only. I did not
receive my driver's license until I was forty seven and a half.

Also, do you think that there will be some accidents with the
change of green and red to now red meaning go?   I think so.
Especially for travelers who are not acquainted with your new
rules.

Please write me back and tell me I am not making a mistake moving
to Omaha. It is a great city and I want to be there. Even with
your crazy lights.

Thanks,

Ted L. Nancy

Public Works Department

Omaha/Douglas Civic Center
1819 Farnam Street, Suite 601
Omaha, Nebraska 68183-0601
(402) 444-5220
Telefax (402) 444-5248

Don W. Elliott, P.E.
Public Works Director

City of Omaha
Hal Daub, Mayor

September 12, 1996

Ted L. Nancy
560 North Moorpark Road #236
Thousand Oaks, CA 91360

Dear Mr. Nancy:

This letter is in regard to your September 5th letter concerning the traffic signal system in the City of Omaha.

The City of Omaha does not have any plans to change the traffic signal system as described in your September 5th letter. Our traffic signal system will stay as it currently exists with green meaning go and red meaning stop.

As a native Omahan, I would like to welcome you to the City of Omaha. I think you will find it is a great City and you will enjoy living here. After you are in Omaha, if you have any questions in regard to traffic, please feel free to contact me.

Sincerely,

Charlie Krajicek, P.E.
Traffic Engineer

c: Laurie Adams, Mayor's Office

jo:document4

560 No. Moorpark Rd. #236
Thousand Oaks, CA 91360

Sep 4, 1996

Appointments
DOCTOR'S FOOT CARE CENTER
The Mall Of Victor Valley
14400 Bear Valley Road
Ste 201
Victorville, CA 92392

Dear Appointments:

I have intensive heel pain. It is so bad that I am ready to slice
my heel off and replace it with my elbow. I only need one elbow.
I just can't do with this heel pain anymore.

Sometimes I throw myself on the floor and roll around in agony.
It is worse than an LSD trip. (I've taken none, but I've seen
several).

Can you help me?

No other part of my body has pain. Only my heel. It is so bad
that I'm blinded by the pain. I have stood on the street and
pointed to my heel with tears running down my face. Yet no one
has stopped.

Please write and tell me what I have to do to schedule an
appointment with you. You are highly recommended by another
person I know who had worse heel pain than I have. He said you
cleared him up in one visit and now he can use his heel.

Also, do you work on parrots? He is hopping. Is it possible I
caught it from him? Thank you for writing with appointment
information. I am ready to bring my heel in.

Sincerely,

Ted L. Nancy

DOCTORS FOOT CARE CENTERS, INC.
A PODIATRY CORPORATION
P.O. Box 3037
Granada Hills, California 91394-0037

September 10, 1996

Dear Mr. Nancy,

Of course we can help you with your heel pain!

I would encourage you to call our Granada Hills office.
That would be closer for you than our Victorville office.
That phone number is (818) 368-2841.

I'm sorry to say, we don't treat parrots. I'm sure there's
a good bird doctor out there. (Maybe he's just having sympathy
pain for you?)

Hope to see you at our Granada Hills office soon.

Sincerely,

Michelle Wade
Office manager
Victorville office
Doctors Foot Care Center, Inc.

GRANADA HILLS TEL. (818) 368-2841 / FAX (818) 368-2290
IRVINE   TEL. (714) 833-3406 / FAX (714) 833-9955
VICTORVILLE   TEL. (619) 951-2000 / FAX (619) 951-2600

560 No. Moorpark Rd. #236
Thousand Oaks, CA 91360

Sep 5, 1996

Records Dept.
AKRON GENERAL MEDICAL CENTER
400 Wabash Ave.
Akron, OH 44307

Dear Records Dept.,

I'll get right to the point. I have a problem. I was in a coma
for 5 years. And when I woke up I found out my wife had left me.
For another man in a coma.

I was in your hospital from 1989 to 1993. I need my records to
give to my paralegal so I can get my wife back. She is now with
this other person who is still in a coma. I am groggy. She just
sits there all day with him. Nothing is going on!   At least I am
up.

Can you please send me my records? My doctor's name at Akron
General is Dr. Jharbdi Del Fudgio. Thanks. I look forward to
hearing from you soon with my medical records.

Sincerely,

Ted L. Nancy

**AKRON GENERAL**
MEDICAL CENTER

Date: _Sept. 10, 1996_

Ted Nancy
560 N. Moorpark #236
Thousand, Oaks, CA 91360

Patient Name:	
Med Rec #:	
RE:	

We are unable to comply with your request(s) for medical information on the above patient as (✔) indicates below. To assist us in locating a record for the above patient, additional information is needed, please furnish the following (✔):

↘ *Print Full Name Below* ↙		
Last	First	Middle
↘ *Other name under which patient may have been treated* ↙		

Date of Birth	
Social Security Number	
Treatment Date	
Admission Date	
Discharge Date	

We require that requests be accompanied by an authorization to release medical information. Authorization must be signed and dated within sixty (60) days of request by patient, legal guardian, if the patient is a minor or, if the patient is deceased, by the appointed executor or administrator of the estate, or if none, by the surviving spouse or next of kin.

☒ *Our computer shows no listing of patient.*

If treated as an outpatient, please direct your requests to the specific department where test(s)/ treatment were performed.

☒ **Other:** _I have checked the area hospitals - no patient treated with this name_

When applicable, please return to:

Medical Record Department, Correspondence Section
AKRON GENERAL MEDICAL CENTER
400 Wabash Avenue
Akron, Ohio 44307

Sincerely,
☺ Medical Record Department

560 North Moorpark Road
Apt #236
Thousand Oaks, CA 91360   USA

Reservations
MERIT ANTIQUE HOTEL
Ordu Cad. 226
Laleli
Istanbul, Turkey   Nov 9, 1996

Dear Merit Antique Reservations:

I want very much to come to Turkey and stay at your beautiful
hotel for 7 nights, Dec 14-20, 1996. I understand you can see the
Bosporus from your room. I also understand there's a small stream
stocked with goldfish running through your lobby. I have the same
thing in my kitchenette. Do you have shoe horns? My shoes are
hard to get on.

JHere (Sometimes I spell 'Here' with a J in front of it; I don't
know why) is my predicament:

I take 9 showers a day. I wake up and take a shower immediately,
then eat my breakfast then take another shower. Then I get
dressed and go out. Before I go out I shower again. Once I am
out for an hour, I return and take another shower. After my lunch
I take a light shower then I take my nap and take a real long hot
shower. I DO NOT shower before dinner. (No time). Before going
to bed I take 3 good, hot, soothing, then cold short, crisp
showers in succession.

I would like maid service after each time I take a shower. That
is a complete bathroom cleaning with tiny soaps, small shampoos, a
shoe horn, and fresh towels. Can this be arranged? I know it is
a lot to ask for but I MUST take these showers, I MUST be clean.
Friends say this about your hotel: The best place to take a
shower is jhere." Is that true?

Please let me know if you have a suite available for Dec 14-20?

Sincerely,

Ted L. Nancy

HOTEL
merit
Antique
ISTANBUL

MR TED L. NANCY   ISTANBUL 21.11.1996
560 N. MOORPARK RD.
#236 THOUSAND OAKS, CA 91360
USA

SUBJECT: RESERVATION REQUEST

Dear Mr NANCY ,

Thank you for your letter and kind interest shown to
Merit Antique Hotel Istanbul.

We can not confirmed your reservation from 14.12.96 to 20.12.
96 Because our hotel is fully booked on this dates.
We do not have Bosporus view, our Hotel is in the old city and
we can not give maid service for your predicament.

Looking forward to welcoming you to HOTEL MERIT ANTIQUE on
your visit to the city of minarets .

Kindest regards,

TULAY SALIHOGLU

560 No. Moorpark Rd. #236
Thousand Oaks, CA 91360

Aug 27, 1996

Personnel Dept.
CITY OF NORFOLK
Dept. Of HR
100 City Hall Bldg., E. Wing
Norfolk, VA 23501

Dear Personnel Dept.:

I was voted Mr. Petite USA in 1983. Can this help me get a job?

I am 5'1" and weigh 108 pounds. I am a tiny man. I wear loose
clothing to appear larger. From a distance I can look 5'2" and
112 pounds.   Some people have even said that (on occasion) I look
like I'm 5'3" 114 pounds but I WILL NOT LIE!!!

Where do I apply for a position in the government sector?

Does the federal government need somebody that was voted Mr.
Petite USA? I am very tiny. I am otherwise a very normal man. I
have some of my hair and a sturdy frame. It's just that I am
considered petite. (Thus the award).

Please write me with info about a petite opening in the federal
government in the state of Virginia. Thanks.

Sincerely,

Ted L. Nancy

City of Norfolk
Department of Human Resources

September 4, 1996

Mr. Ted L. Nancy
560 No. Moorpark Rd. # 236
Thousand Oaks, CA 91360

Dear Mr. Nancy:

I have received your request for information on employment. My response is limited to consideration for with the City of Norfolk.

In order to be considered for employment you submit a City of Norfolk employment application for those positions in which you are interested. We post all of our current vacancies via telephone (804-664-4010, code 353) and computer bulletin board (804-664-4466). I have taken the liberty of enclosing three such applications

Thank you for your inquiry. Should you have additional questions concerning employment with the City of Norfolk, please contact me at (804)664-4461.

Kindest regards,

Eddie P. Antoine, II
Human Resources Manager

560 No. Moorpark Rd. #236
Thousand Oaks, CA 91360

Mar 10, 1997

Bulk Sales Department
ECW PRESS
2120 Queen St. E., Suite 200
Toronto, Ontario
M4E 1E2
Canada

Dear Bulk Sales Dept.,

I am interested in bulk sales of your book, "PARTY MIDGET." The
book about a midget who likes to party, if you know what I mean.

I would like to buy 215 books for our TALL CLUB. This is a group
of men who have a club because they are tall. Everyone wants to
read this book. It has been discussed.

Several members have recently acquired a midget fetish and are
thinking about leaving our club. Naturally, you can understand
our concern. We would like to read "Party Midget" to see if there
is anything to this fetish. Perhaps we may become the TALL AND
SMALL CLUB. Maybe, but I am reminded of the painful fable "THE
LABRADOR AND THE CHIHUAHUA." Also, do you have that book? We
need 191 copies of that.

Please send all correspondence to: Me. I anxiously await "Party
Midget" and "The Labrador And The Chihuahua."

Or, if you can recommend a book for our club we would be more than
interested. I was told that your company publishes this book and
other interesting books. Thank you.

Sincerely,

Ted L. Nancy

560 No. Moorpark Rd #236
Thousand Oaks, CA 91360

Aug 1, 1996

BUREAU OF ENGRAVING AND PRINTING
DEPT OF THE TREASURY
14th and C Streets, SW
Washington, DC 20228

Dear Bureau of Engraving and Printing,

I have just found out that you will be removing Abraham Lincoln's
face from the five dollar bill and will be showing a picture of
him from the waist down. Why?

I see no need to show his legs, knees and possibly feet not to
mention his waist area. I think this could be obscene and vulgar
if not done tastefully.

Plus, it could be any president. Only a person with knowledge of
Lincoln's waist would know. And how many of them are left?

I know Lincoln was a tall man and there was plenty of him to go
around but why the need to show his midsection on the five dollar
bill? We don't even see his neck now. Why not just add the neck?

Please let me know that my fears are unfounded and this is not
true. That you WILL NOT be showing Lincoln's waist on the five
dollar bill. Thank you for getting back to me on this pressing
matter.

Sincerely,

Ted L. Nancy

Nicola Winstanley
Associate Editor

E C W   P R E S S

2120 Queen Street East, Suite 200, Toronto, Ontario, Canada M4E 1E2
Telephone (416) 694-3348   *Fax* (416) 698-9906

560 Moorpark Road. #236
Thousand Oaks, CA 91360

March 26, 1997

Dear Ted L. Nancy,

Thankyou for your amusing letter!! Unfortunately we do not publish the book
"Party Midget," nor "The Labrador and the Chihuahua," at ECW. Good luck in
finding out who does!

Yours sincerely

Nicola Winstanley
Associate Editor

DEPARTMENT OF THE TREASURY
BUREAU OF ENGRAVING AND PRINTING
WASHINGTON, D.C. 20228

AUG 1 2 1996

Mr. Ted L. Nancy
560 No. Moorpark Road, #236
Thousand Oaks, CA 91360

Dear Mr. Nancy:

This is in response to your August 1, 1996, letter concerning rumors you've heard that Abraham Lincoln's face would be removed from the $5 note when it is redesigned.

What you've heard is absolutely false. There is no such plan and this agency prints all U.S. paper currency.

Sincerely,

Claudia W. Dickens
Public Affairs Specialist

560 No. Moorpark Rd #236
Thousand Oaks, CA 91360

Sep 30, 1996

Customer Service
JOHNSON'S ODOR EATERS
White Plains, NY 10604

Dear Odor Eaters,

I want to join ODOR EATERS ANONYMOUS. I have heard that your
organization does wonderful things for those that can't control
their foot smell.

My feet smell so bad, I am forced to eat out by the garbage
dumpster area when dining out. What can I do?   Please help me.
Does eating garlic, onions, mango sauce, and old bologna affect
your feet smell?

When are the meetings?   Can I get a ride?   I have a Ford
Fairlane. But I may buy a Mercury Topaz.

Please send me all information regarding Odor Eaters Anonymous. I
mean I want ALL information; as much as I can get. Don't hold
back.

Also do you make corn holders? I have corns on my feet that I
understand you make a colorful corn holder for. Do these need to
be installed by a professional, or can I attach them myself?
Please send me a picture of your corn holder. Thank you for
writing back with information for me.

Thank you for caring about the feet stink of others.

Sincerely,

Ted L. Nancy

Combe

incorporated

White Plains, N.Y. 10604-3597
Telephone: (914) 694-5454
Fax: (914) 694-6320

October 7, 1996

Mr. Ted L. Nancy
560 N. Moorpark Road #236
Thousand Oaks, CA 91360

Dear Mr. Nancy:

Thank you for your letter concerning **Johnson's Ultra-Comfort ODOR-EATERS Insoles.** We were very pleased to learn that you are interested in our product.

Odor-Eaters combine cushion-soft latex foam with millions of tiny particles of activated charcoal which actually trap and remove odor and perspiration from the feet, the socks and the shoes. The remarkable purifying and filtration properties of activated charcoal is the secret which makes Odor-Eaters so highly effective. This purifying and filtration property is the same principle which was used in the Apollo spaceship and is used in the nuclear submarines to keep air pure.

There is no stereotype person that may have foot odor. We are enclosing a pamphlet, "Save your feet..." which may answer some of the questions you have concerning foot odor. It also contains some valuable store coupons for future purchases of our **ODOR-EATERS** line of insoles.

Your continued interest in **ODOR-EATERS** is greatly appreciated.

Very truly yours,

Stephanie Medina
Consumer Affairs Consultant

SM:co
ENC:bklt
0017j
OE/16c

560 No. Moorpark Rd. #236
Thousand Oaks, CA 91360

Aug 22, 1996

Wedding Planner
A PRECIOUS MOMENT WEDDING CHAPEL
800 South 4th St.
Las Vegas, NV 89101

Dear Wedding Planner,

My intended wife and I want to be married at your chapel on
September 29, 1996.

We have a fantasy. We want to consummate our marriage in the
chapel office immediately after the wedding ceremony. We will be
in there for approximately 45 minutes, maybe an hour.

We will only touch your desk, couch (or 2 chairs), and, of course,
the floor. We are clean people, no diseases. We will not leave
any mess in your office and we WILL put down a plastic protective
spalsh over your desk, couch, etc. Nothing will be messed.

Naturally we will compensate you for our consummation. Money is
not the issue here. It is our desire to wed and consummate our
marriage as one ceremony.

Please let us know what the charge would be to have our ceremony
climaxed in your office. We are willing to pay what is necessary
for this service. You can schedule us any time of the day or
evening so we won't disrupt your business.

Please write and tell us how much for your wedding package on
September 29, 1996. Thank you very much. I look forward to a
speedy reply so we can make our wedding plans immediately.

Sincerely,

Ted L. Nancy

A Precious Moment
Wedding Chapel

800 South Fourth Street • Las Vegas, NV 89101
(702) 384-2211 • 1-800-9-MARRY U • FAX 384-2232

August 28, 1996

Ted L. Nancy
560 N. Moorpark Rd.
#236
Thousand Oaks, CA 91360

Dear Mr. Nancy:

   Thank you for your inquiry of Aug. 22, 1996.

   Enclosed find a "Package Price List" stating our services in the chapel. None of these include the chapel offices for consumation of marriage purposes.

   There are many hotels downtown nearby the chapel where you can book your lodging. Our limousine driver will return you immediately after your wedding ceremony for your con-sumation of marriage.

   Should this be satisfactory with you and your bride, call and schedule your wedding.

Yours Truly,

Betty Williams
GENERAL MANAGER

BJW/dw

♥ Where Love's Dreams Come True ♥

560 No. Moorpark Rd. #236
Thousand Oaks, CA 91360

Nov 20, 1996

MS. BETTY WILLIAMS
A PRECIOUS MOMENT WEDDING CHAPEL
800 South Fourth St.
Las Vegas, NV 89109

Dear MS. Williams,

Thank you for answering my letter regarding the fantasy my future
wife and I have of having sex in your office. I am sorry I am
tardy in writing back but I had an accident and lost three of my
toes.

Naturally, your suggestion about returning to our hotel is nice
but it does not satisfy my wife's (or my) fantasy. And she needs
to be satisfied. We have chosen the Precious Moment Wedding
Chapel because of the good things we hear about it and, of course,
the fact that it MAY be possible to have our wedding consummated
in your office.

In your brochure you include the "other" option. Our request
would certainly fall under "other." So what do you say? Let's
put convention behind us - get some oils and towels - and get it
on in your office.

Please let me know if there is ANY FEE, no matter how large, that
you would consider for our wedding night. Thank you. I look
forward to hearing from you as we do want to form our union soon.

Sincerely,

Ted L. Nancy

A PRECIOUS MOMENT CHAPEL
800 S. 4TH STREET
LAS VEGAS, NV 89101

Nov. 29, 1996

Ted L. Nancy
560 N. Moorpark Rd. #236
Thousand Oaks, CA 91360

Dear Mr. Nancy:

Received your correspondence of Nov. 20, 1996. We do sympathize with you and your bride regarding your fanciful whimsy for connubial consummation in my center for administ-rative directives...oils and towels notwithstanding.

Unfortunately it will not be possible for your wedding consummation to take place in my office. So, you can be married in our chapel and [BLEEP] somewhere else or find a chapel in sympathy with your deviate desires.

Sincerely,

B. Williams

PS Regret your latest accident in losing three toes...the
   one before must have been a bump on the head. With all
   our advances in therapy and modern medicine, I feel con-
   fident you can have complete recovery. Of which a sure
   sign would be an understanding of the sanctity of
   marriage.

WASTE IS A TERRIBLE THING TO MIND

MY CONTINUING JOB SEARCH

Ted L. Nancy
560 No. Moorpark Rd. #236
Thousand Oaks, CA 91360

Business Permits
CITY OF WALNUT CREEK
1666 N. Main St.
Walnut Creek, CA 94596   Sep 27, 1996

Dear Business Permits Dept.:

I need a business permit. I have a van where I stop and open a
door and a red haired man steps out. He will wash his hands and
towel off and adjust his trousers. I charge $12.00 for this
(which includes a papaya slice) and drive around your
neighborhoods.

I need to get a license to do this in your city. I also need a
van, a towel, squeeze soap, papaya slices, and a red haired man.
Can you help me with this? (Frizzy red hair and freckles,
please).

Thank you, Walnut Creek. I want to now bring my van to your
streets so everyone can enjoy this red haired man washing his
hands and toweling off. I look forward to a prompt reply.

Sincerely,

Ted L. Nancy

Ted L. Nancy

city of Walnut Creek

October 25, 1996

Ted L. Nancy
560 No. Moorpark Rd. #236
Thousand Oaks, Ca 91360

We are pleased that you intend or are currently doing business within our City of Walnut Creek.

Our records indicate that you have not yet filed for your business license so I am enclosing an application for your convenience.

Please complete the enclosed application in detail and return to this office with the appropriate tax. You may choose either Option A or B from the schedule of taxes found on the reverse side of the application. Business Tax is due and payable from date of your beginning business in Walnut Creek through the end of our fiscal year on June 30 and thereafter due annually on July 1.

Paying promptly will avoid penalties (required by Municipal Code) that amass at 10% per month up to 50% of business license taxes.

Revenue derived from business license taxes supports our Police, Public Service, Community Development, Cultural Services and General Government.

A copy of the Municipal Code covering business licenses is available upon request.

Thank you for your prompt cooperation.

Eve Feiler
Business License Coordinator

560 No. Moorpark Rd. #236
Thousand Oaks, CA 91360

Nov 13, 1997

Licensing Office
CITY OF BILLINGS
2330 5th Ave. S.
Billings, MT 59101

Dear License Bureau:

Soon I will open "Nostrils By The Bay - Premier Belgian Cuisine."
I will cater to the upscale diners and have dancing, valet
parking, and a sketch artist that will draw people while they eat.

Please advise on how I get a license. I will erect a 50 foot
Nostrils sign where people walk in through openings. It will be
the largest free standing Nostrils sign in Montana. Only Florida
has one bigger.

I look forward to hearing from you with my permit information
soon. And please stop by and try our new Lions Club Sandwich.
The B.L.T. Bacon, lion, and tomato. Complimentary, of course.

Thank you,

Ted L. Nancy

CITY-COUNTY HEALTH DEPARTMENT
123 SOUTH 27TH STREET
PHONE (406) 247-3200   FAX (406) 247-3202

P.O. BOX 35033
BILLINGS, MT
59107-5033

ENVIRONMENTAL HEALTH COURTHOUSE--RM 308 PO BOX 35035 BILLINGS, MT 59107
(406) 256-2770   FAX (406) 256-2767

November 24, 1997

Ted L. Nancy
560 North Moorpark Road #236
Thousand Oaks, CA 91360

Re: Food Service License
Nostrils By The Bay

Dear Mr. Nancy:

Thank you for your inquiry regarding food service establishment licenses and review information required in Billings. I have enclosed the rules for food service establishments in Montana. A set of plans and specifications will be required for review by this office before the start of construction. The review fee is $35.00. If an on-site evaluation of an existing structure is required this office will be available to conduct an evaluation at your convenience.

A food purveyor license of $60.00 from the Department of Public Health and Human Services is required. This office issues the license before opening the establishment. There is also a City of Billings business license of $105.00 when operating within the city limits of Billings.

The City of Billings Building Department (406-657-8270) should be contacted if construction is required. Brian Anderson is the plan reviewer.

If this office can assist you with further information please contact us at 256-2770.

Sincerely yours,

Gary Bradshaw, R.S.

cc: Reading File
       File

560 No. Moorpark Rd. #236
Thousand Oaks, CA 91360

Feb 19, 1997

SEARS
233 South Wacker Drive
Chicago, IL 60684

Dear Sears:

I am the creator of the "FURWACKER" electric BEAST SHAVER. Mine
is the only beast shaver that works on all mammals and some large
birds. (No cranes, please!).

Being in the business, I'm sure you're aware of my difficulties.
My "FurWacker" Beast Shaver is now available for licensing, and
from my past dealings with Sears, (I bought a tire and some
socks), I feel obligated to offer you the first opportunity to
license the rights. (Plus you're on Wacker Drive - is this fate?)

Many people care for unusual creatures. Did you know some states
sell prairie ferrets as pets? Without Mother Nature, and I'm
emphatic about this, even a hamster must be shaved. Also, I'm
proud to say: During development NO guinea pigs were used as
guinea pigs.

The "FurWacker" is almost silent, featuring a purr sound causing
MOST creatures to be still. (Except cranes).

So, Sears, please tell me how I may get this into your stores so
that soon it is the Kenmore FurWacker Beast Shaver?

Thank you. I look forward to your reply. Hey, whatever happened
to Roebuck? You never hear about him anymore.

Respectfully,

Ted L. Nancy

Phil Samuelson
Director Nat'l Customer Relations
D/727CCR   E4-111B

Sears, Roebuck and Co.
3333 Beverly Road
Hoffman Estates, Illinois 60179

March 7, 1997

Mr. Ted L. Nancy
560 N. Moorpark Rd. #236
Thousand Oaks, CA 91360

Dear Mr. Nancy:

Thank you for your submittal regarding your product (Furwacker). We deeply
appreciate that you have considered Sears to market or utilize your product.

As you are probably aware, each year we receive thousands of unsolicited proposals
from individuals, companies and other outside sources desiring to do business with
Sears. Unfortunately, like your product, they don't always meet our current marketing
needs.

Thank you again for the interest you have shown.

Very truly yours,

Phil Samuelson
Director Nat'l Customer Relations

PS:lp

560 No. Moorpark Rd. #236
Thousand Oaks, CA 91360

Aug 10, 1996

Administration
CITY OF ANAHEIM
200 S. Anaheim Blvd.
Suite 332
Anaheim, CA 92805

Dear City of Anaheim:

I am building a small business in the shape of your Anaheim
airport. Mine will be a hair care shop and pet bath business. I
may sell pet ointment. Maybe salve.

I was told to write to the city of Anaheim so that I may get
permission and proceed with my business that will look like your
Anaheim airport.

Can you please direct me so that I may get the paperwork started?
I am anxious to get my business going. Hair care and pet baths
are very important in this area (plenty of pets) and I can't
proceed unless I get the permission to use your airport as my
reproduction.

Thank you very much. I look forward to hearing from you soon. I
have always thought the Anaheim airport was a model of efficiency.
Tell me where I get the paperwork.

Respectfully,

Ted L. Nancy
Ted L. Nancy

August 12, 1996

Ted L. Nancy
560 N. Moorpark Rd. #236
Thousand Oaks, CA 91360

Dear Mr. Nancy:

This is in response to your letter dated August 10, 1996, regarding the
reproduction of an airport to model your business. Although your idea is very
appealing, unfortunately, the City of Anaheim does not have an airport. However,
a municipal airport is located in the City of Fullerton, and the Orange County John
Wayne Airport is located in the City of Costa Mesa. I hope this will be of some
help to you.

I appreciate your interest in our city, and hope you will find a model for your
business.

Sincerely,

David M. Morgan
Assistant City Manager

DMM/ir

560 North Moorpark Road.
Suite 236
Thousand Oaks, Cal 91360

Business Permits
CITY OF SANTA MONICA
1685 Main St
Santa Monica, CA 90407   Aug 9, 1996

Dear Business Permits Dept:

I am interested in obtaining a business permit.

I own "TED L. NANCY'S CLEAN UNDERWEAR KIOSK." I sell clean
underwear from a kiosk. I want to place 65 of them around the
city.

You ever get to the mall and say I want to change my underwear?
Now you can do it from my clean underwear kiosk. There is no need
to go home, change your underwear, and come back. How many times
do you want to go to an important business dinner? Wouldn't a
change of clean underwear be nice?

I have a changing screen where you can change your underwear and
even leave your 'dirties' where they will be disposed of. (Need
information on this. Rules, county dumpage, etc.).

I am interested in setting up my "CLEAN UNDERWEAR KIOSK" in your
malls and airports and at night by your music centers and theater
districts. Clean underwear creates foot traffic! I sell fresh,
personally supervised, hand crafted, pre washed underwear
competitively priced, sizes petite to triple XXX 61 waist.

Can you please tell me how I get permission to do this? What
permits I need, paperwork to fill out, etc.

I also operate an adjacent frankfurter stand and feature a daily
"UNDERWEAR AND LUNCH SPECIAL." One classic brief and a krautdog
for five bucks is the most popular.

What is the process for me to have a mobile underwear and hot dog
business in your city? I look forward to a wonderfully symbiotic
relationship.

Respectfully,

Ted L. Nancy

CITY OF
SANTA MONICA
CALIFORNIA

BUSINESS LICENSE OFFICE
1685 Main Street
P.O. Box 2200
Santa Monica, CA 90407-2200
Telephone (310) 458-8745
Fax (310) 394-2962

August 19, 1996

Ted L. Nancy
560 North Moorpark Rd.
Thousand Oaks, CA 91360

Dear Mr. Nancy,

The License Office is in receipt of your letter requesting
information regarding licensing a hot dog cart and clean
underwear kiosk in the City of Santa Monica.

The Zoning Code only allows outdoor sales activity on Third
Street Promenade, the Santa Monica Pier, and six locations bided
on in a lottery program every two years. Carts are only allowed
on Third Street Promenade through a cart program administered by
the Bayside District, and requires Planning approval and a
Business License, for more information on the Third Street
Promenade cart program please call (310) 393-8355. Currently, the
Santa Monica Pier is not taking any applications and the next
lottery will be held February 1998.

If you have a location inside a building the enclosed brochure
explains the Business License and Planning procedure.

If you have any questions please call the License Office at (310)
458-8745.

Sincerely,

Debra Sowers
License & Permit Supervisor

(nancy)

560 No. Moorpark Rd. #236
Thousand Oaks, CA 91360

Sep 5, 1996

Submissions Dept.
PENGUIN USA PUBLISHING COMPANY
375 Hudson Street
New York, NY 10014

Dear Submissions Dept.:

I have a book that I'm sure you will want to read. I believe I
have been examined by Aliens. I was probed, touched, examined and
searched. All this was done in a bush.

My story is real! Only myself, and the aliens know the truth.
(Maybe a leaf blower man). Are you interested in reading the
entire story from the supermarket parking lot to a pet store
alley? I am almost finished with the manuscript now.

I am on chapter 61 where I was taken aboard the mother craft, my
pants taken down, my area washed, (and noted in a journal), and
then released after being examined, probed, and tickled. I was
then taken to the bush where the study was finished. I enjoyed
everything but the tickling.

I have pictures that were taken then given to me. People looking
at them are startled.

THIS IS A TRUE STORY. I believe this book could be very
educational to high school students and others. Everyone should
read this book. This is a authentic account of my visit with the
other world.

Please let me know if you are interested in looking at my pictures
of me being tickled?   Thank you.

Sincerely,

Ted L. Nancy

Penguin USA

375 Hudson Street
New York, NY 10014

Telephone 212-366-2000
Fax 212-366-2666

January 30, 1997

Ted L. Nancy
560 Moorpark
#236
Thousand Oaks, CA 91360

Dear Mr. Nancy,

Thank you for taking an interest in Viking Penguin. Your story of alien abduction sounds quite fascinating. As we're sure you know, we receive many hundreds of requests from people who want to have their stories published by our company, and are unable to publish them all.

However, we are willing to consider whatever material you would like to submit. Please include the photos (or color copies of them) so that we can determine the validity of your account.

Send to:

ARKANA
Viking Penguin
375 Hudson St.
New York, NY 10012

We look forward to receiving your material.

Best regards,

The Editorial Department

A Pearson Company

560 No. Moorpark Rd. #236
Thousand Oaks, CA 91360

Aug 22, 1996

City Office
CITY OF LEWISVILLE
1197 W Main
Lewisville, TX 75067

Dear City Of Lewisville:

I am sure that I am in possession of a "deed of grant" from the
transitional government of the "New State Of Texas" that verifies
I own all the land for what you call Lewisville.

Naturally, I don't want to throw the good people of Lewisville out
of my land. You have the best Sizzler!   However, I do want to
change the name to Perry King. The city of Lewisville will in
effect be now known as Perry King, Texas, 75067

Who can I communicate with regarding my ownership of the city of
Lewisville?   I have a legal document signed giving me ownership
to this land.

I just would like to show my deed to someone. It says TED L.
NANCY OWNS LEWISVILLE, TEXAS. I am looking at it now. I keep it
in my refrigerator for safekeeping. It is moist, but still
readable. Please write and tell me what office I should
communicate with regarding my claim. Thank you for getting back
to me on this.

Sincerely,

Ted L. Nancy

I love your Sizzler!

August 27, 1996

The Honorable Ted L. Nancy
560 N. Moorpark Road, #236
Thousand Oaks, California 91360

Dear Mr. Nancy:

Congratulations! It has recently come to my attention that you are now the legal owner of the city of Perry King, Texas, formerly known as Lewisville, Texas, by virtue of a deed of grant from the transitional government of the *New State of Texas*.

As I have been intrigued with how this venture was accomplished, I am writing to you today to request information on how I, too, may obtain a city in Texas through the transitional government of the *New State of Texas*.

I would appreciate obtaining a list of all available cities and towns in Texas, as I want to own a good one.   Please be so kind to send this information to me in the envelope provided.

After you respond, and conditioned upon the fact I am able to achieve this goal, I will then share with you my ideas to form a "townowners association" for membership of owners of cities and towns in the *New State of Texas*.

Thank you for your favor in reply.

Sincerely,

Atina Noslen

PS: I would advise you to keep all important documents in a place other than a refrigerator (they could mold).

560 No. Moorpark Rd. #236
Thousand Oaks, Ca 91360

Sep 27, 1996

Business Permits
CITY OF LONG BEACH
333 W. Ocean Blvd.
Long Beach, CA 90802

Dear Business Permits Dept.:

I need to get a business permit from you to operate my SUMO VAN in
the city of Long Beach. I am moving there soon.

My Sumo Van operates like this: My van stops, the doors slide
open, and two 500 pound sumo wrestlers each slap their belly
against the other. They grunt and groan and break into a sweat
while an audience watches. Everyone loves it!

I charge $5.50 a person.   This is good family entertainment. It
is something to see, these big wrestlers wearing their tiny sumo
lap cloths slapping each other around with their big stomachs.
They really go at it. Dogs bark.

Please tell me how I go about getting a permit to operate my Sumo
Van on your city streets?   I may place 16 vans around your city
roaming up and down the streets. At its height, I could have 32
sumo wrestlers belly bumping each other with their girth. Thank
you.

Sincerely,

Ted L. Nancy

Ted L. Nancy

CITY OF LONG BEACH
DEPARTMENT OF FINANCIAL MANAGEMENT

333 West Ocean Boulevard · Long Beach, CA 90802 · (310) 570-6024 · FAX (310) 570-5260

October 8, 1996

Ted L. Nancy
560 N. Moorpark Road #236
Thousand Oaks, CA 91360

Dear Mr. Nancy:

Thank you for your letter dated September 27, 1996, regarding your interest in establishing a sumo wrestling van business in the City of Long Beach. Unfortunately the type of business activity you wish to establish is not permitted on public streets in Long Beach. Should you wish to establish a fixed location to promote sumo wrestling, you must first obtain zoning approval from the Planning and Building Department. You would also be required to obtain City Council approval to conduct any wrestling event in the City of Long Beach.

If you have any questions regarding this matter, please contact Jaunice Floyd, Business License Supervisor, at (310) 570-6211.

Sincerely,

PATTY HEINTZELMAN
Business Services Officer
Commercial Services Bureau

PH:lh
sumo.ltr

ADMINISTRATIVE SERVICES
(310) 570-5045
Fax (310) 570-5099

BUDGET MANAGEMENT
(310) 570-6425
Fax (310) 570-5260

CITY CONTROLLER
(310) 570-6450
Fax (310) 570-6760

CITY TREASURER
(310) 570-6845
Fax (310) 570-6645

COMMERCIAL SERVICES
(310) 570-7031
Fax (310) 570-6867

Ted L. Nancy
560 No. Moorpark Rd. #236
Thousand Oaks, CA 91360

Mar 3, 1997

NBA COMMISSIONER MR. DAVID STERN
National Basketball Association
Olympic Tower, 645 Fifth Avenue
New York, NY 10022

Dear Commissioner Stern,

I have developed the **VLADE DIVAC SPANKPADDLE**. I'm sure you'll
agree, sometimes all a wrongdoer needs is a good old fashioned
spanking to put them on track. And nothing will do it better than
an NBA approved Vlade Divac Spankpaddle. (Formally called the
Slappy). I can't think of anyone Americans have more respect for,
or wouldn't mind getting a swat from, than Mr. Divac. He's
America's dad!   (Now that Ed Asner is not on TV anymore).

I am currently involved in a bidding war with several major
companies regarding the manufacturing of the SPANKPADDLE. It also
has an attachment for naughty pets.

How about a commercial showing the Miami Heat standing in line for
their Vlade Divac spanking? That'll teach 'em respect. It's a
great message. How about a farm system for basketball players
that don't go to college?   I would love to spearhead that.

Please let me know how I may send this Spankpaddle to you for NBA
approval? I am sending one to Vlade Divac.

I look forward to hearing from you soon. You are doing a great
job with the drug induced, sex fiend players of the National
Basketball Association. It is nice to know that you are clean and
in charge.

How do I get tickets for this year's NBA finals?

Respectfully,

Ted L. Nancy

Ted L. Nancy

National Basketball Association

March 19, 1997

Ted L. Nancy
560 No. Moorpark Rd. #236
Thousand Oaks , CA 91360

Dear Ted:

I am responding to your recent letter to the National Basketball Association regarding game tickets.

Please contact the team of your choice to obtain tickets as they are not sold or distributed through the league office. Unfortunately there is nothing the league office can do in the event of a sellout.

Thank you for your interest in the NBA.

Cordially,

Jennifer Norris

Jennifer Norris
Interactive Services

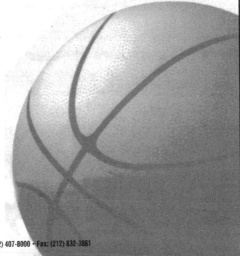

560 No. Moorpark Rd. #236
Thousand Oaks, CA 91360

Feb 25, 1997

Business Permits Division
City Hall
CITY OF LEWISVILLE
123 NE 1 Terr
Lewisville, AR 71845

Dear Business Permits Division:

I need a permit to operate my business in your city.

So many businesses today are done from the home. In today's world
of people working out of their homes, I offer this:

I will clean your home from my home.

This is the perfect solution to those too busy to do their own
cleaning. I do bathrooms, windows (and screens) and even your
porch. All from my home. When you arrive home your house is
spotless and I haven't left my house. If you're not satisfied
call me. I'll be at home.

Write and tell me how I get a business permit for this. Thank
you.

Sincerely,

Ted L. Nancy

Ted L. Nancy

CITY OF LEWISVILLE—LEWISVILLE, ARKANSAS

2nd & Murphy
P. O. Box 70
LEWISVILLE, ARKANSAS 71845

Phone 921-4971

March 18, 1997

Ted L. Nancy,

I have researched this matter and to my knowledge and the Mayor's knowledge there is no need to obtain a permit for your business in Lewisville, Arkansas.

If you have any further questions please do not hesitate to contact myself or Mayor Fletcher.

Sincerely,

Laurie Brady, City Clerk/Treasurer

560 No. Moorpark Rd. #236
Thousand Oaks, CA 91360

Sep 4, 1996

Job Information
DEPARTMENT OF STATE
2201 C Street NW
Washington, D.C. 20520

Dear Sir or Madam:

I pride myself on having exact change. When I leave the house I
try to estimate EXACTLY what the cost of something is and regulate
my change as thus.

For the last 16 years I have left my home estimating the exact
change I would need for everything I do including parking, lunch,
toiletries, laundry, bus fair, mints, etc. I AM NEVER WRONG!!

I have been a consultant to the private efficiency industry now
looking for a government position.

What government jobs are currently open in the exact change
industry?   If not, are there any related exact change jobs
currently open?   What about exact paper bills but not correct
change?   Where can I fill out the forms?

Certainly the State Department can use someone that has exact
change CONSTANTLY on a continuous basis. I look forward to
hearing from you soon regarding my job search in the federal exact
change sector. Thank you.

Sincerely,

Ted L. Nancy

Ted L. Nancy

United States Department of State

Washington, D.C.   20520

Thank you for your recent inquiry to the U.S. Department of State requesting information on a career as a Foreign Service Specialist. The following positions are **currently open**:

Facilities Maintenance Specialist	FP-04	$36,870 - $44,025
	FP-05	$29,876 - $35,674
	FP-06	$26,708 - $31,891
Information Management Technical Specialist - Telephone (IMTS-T 95-1)	FP-05	$32,646 - $38,981
	FP-06	$29,185 - $34,848
Information Management Technical Specialist - Radio (IMTS-R 95-1)	FP-05	$32,646 - $38,981
	FP-06	$29,185 - $34,848
Information Management Technical Specialist - Computer (IMTS-C 95-1)	FP-05	$32,646 - $38,981
	FP-06	$29,185 - $34,848
Information Management Technical Specialist - Digital (IMTS-D 95-1)	FP-05	$32,646 - $38,981
	FP-06	$29,185 - $34,848

The following positions are **closed**:

Communications Electronics Officer
Construction Engineering Officer
Diplomatic Courier
Diplomatic Security Officer/Special Agent **
Financial Management Officer
Foreign Service Secretary
General Services Officer

Information Management Specialist
Medical Officer/Psychiatrist *
Medical Technologist *
Narcotics Control Officer
Nurse Practitioner *
Personnel Officer
Security Engineering Officer

Current information on these and other Foreign Service Specialist positions is available by calling our Career Line at (703) 875-7490.

*For information on the medical positions, please contact Ms. Rita Torchia at (202) 663-1750.

**Opening in October 1996.

Thank you for your interest in a career with the U.S. Department of State.

Visit our Web Site at: http:\\www.state.gov (click on careers)

WALT'S AIRPORT MATTRESS SHOP
ONLY KING SIZE MATTRESSES: ONLY AT THE AIRPORT

560 No. Moorpark Rd. #236
Thousand Oaks, Calif 91360 USA

Mar 14, 1997

Leasing Dept.
TURKISH INTERNATIONAL AIRPORT
Esenboga Airport
Ankara, Turkey

Dear Airport Leasing Dept.:

I want to open a branch of my chain: "Walt's Mattress Shop" at
your airport. I sell only king size mattresses and only to
travelers. So if you're at the airport and you want to buy a
mattress come in.

We offer only the finest king size mattresses. They are made with
cobbler's straw just like the old school. We keep our prices low
because we take away the frills: No checks or credit cards,
please. Strictly cash and carry. No delivery services, no sales
people. No lifting on our part. (We DO NOT put your mattress on
the plane!)

Just stop in, choose your mattress, get it from one of the top
four shelves, put it in a bag, give us the cash, and take it away.
It's as simple as that.

Usually we are located between the Ultimate Cashew Store and the
ladies room. Please tell me how I may lease airport space from
you. (DO NOT mistake us for "Walt's Airport Swimming Pool Tarps."
We are not them!) I look forward to a prompt reply. Thank you.

Sincerely,

Ted L. Nancy
Ted L. Nancy

DEVLET HAVA MEYDANLARI İŞLETMESİ
GENEL MÜDÜRLÜĞÜ
ESENBOĞA
HAVA LİMANI BAŞMÜDÜRLÜĞÜ

Sayı :

Özü :

18. 7. 1992

Dear Sir,

    We have received to your letter. But unfortunately we have no space at our airport to lease since our terminal buildings are little and narrow.

There fore we have to give negative answer to you regardless what business you'd like to do.

Best Regards
A.Naci İŞIK
AIRPORT DIRECTOR

INTERMISSION

PLEASE USE THIS TIME NOW TO FRESHEN UP
OR MAKE A SANDWICH

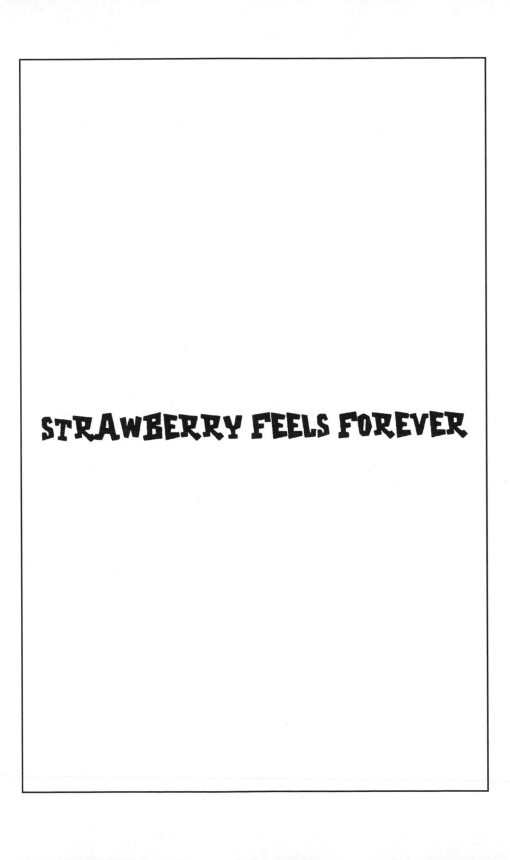

STRAWBERRY FEELS FOREVER

560 No. Moorpark Rd.
#236
Thousand Oaks, CA 91360

Oct 21, 1996

MS. Mariana Tilton
NORMANDIE CASINO & SHOWROOM
Vegas In L.A.
1045 W. Rosecrans Ave.
Gardenia, CA 90247

Dear MS. Tilton:

I am a 675 pound look a like for George Harrison. I am in a group
called the "FAT BEATLES."

We have a tubby Paul who is 490 pounds. He is the cute fat
Beatle. We have a huge John - 751 pounds and gaining. Could be
800 pounds by time of show. We may have to put him in something
other than our collarless Beatle jacket as he cannot fit now. Yet
he really wails as a fleshy John. Our drummer is a 585 pound
Ringo. The girls go nuts when he woo woos and shakes his head.
He has to be lifted onto his drum stool.

Do you want to see our tape? We sing for 90 minutes then answer
questions on what it's like to be a FAT BEATLE. We are the best!

Sometimes we have a thin Bachman Turner Overdrive open for us.
(Can get in touch with them if you are interested). They are rail
thin - less then 100 pounds each. They're "SKINNY BTO." We have
a tape.

Please let me know how the FAT BEATLES can play your theater?
This is an act who's time has come. I look forward to hearing
from you soon. You should really see this tape.

Sincerely,

Ted L. Nancy

George

Resort Entertainment
A NEDERLANDER EVENT

October 30, 1996

Mr. Ted L. Nancy
560 N. Moorpark Rd.
Thousand Oaks, CA 91360

Dear Mr. Nancy:

I heard about the "Fat Beatles" from Mariana Tilton at the Normandie Casino, an account of mine. I would very much like you to send me a tape ASAP. This sounds like it could be a very enjoyable and profitable project.

Sincerely,

Marc Berman

560 No. Moorpark Rd #236
Thousand Oaks, CA 91360

8/28/96

Administration
CITY OF STOCKTON
2500 Navy Drive
Stockton, CA 95202

Dear City Planners,

I understand the city of Stockton is sponsoring PETE BEST DAY in
recognition of the former Beatle and the contribution he has made
to Beatlemania. Without Pete Best, we may have had a different
Ringo.

I am a fan of Pete Best going way back to Germany when he was
known as the hot dog from Hamburg. I think this event is far
overdue and I can imagine Pete Best thinks it's far overdue. He
must be simmering. I saw him at the airport once and he was
grimacing. This man has had some restraint! He had held himself
in for 33 years and now deserves his own event!

Please let me know when PETE BEST DAY will be taking place? I
would like info on Stockton hotels, transportation, clothing,
tickets, laundry service, egg salad sandwiches, Beatle wigs, and
eyeglass repair shops. Thanks.

I look forward to hearing from you soon as I have to travel to
Stockton and make arrangements.

Sincerely

Ted L. Nancy

**SAN JOAQUIN
CONVENTION & VISITORS BUREAU**

17 September 1996

Ted L. Nancy
560 N. Moorpark Road, #236
Thousand Oaks, CA 91360

Dear Mr. Nancy,

Thank you for contacting the City of Stockton concerning PETE BEST DAY.

Unfortunately their is no recognization of the former Beatle going on in the Stockton area to our knowledge.

I have also checked with the San Francisco Convention & Visitor's Bureau and they have not heard of any recognization, either.

If we can be of further assistance to you, please contact us.

Sincerely,

Loralee McGaughey,
Office Manager

560 No. Moorpark Rd.
Apt #236
Thousand Oaks, CA 91360
USA

MR. RINGO STARR
2 Glynde Mews
London SW3 1SB England   9/23/96

Dear Ringo,

I'm in serious need of a pep talk from you. I'd like you to give
me a solid talking to. I am desperately in need of an individual
gusto talk from a qualified celebrity like yourself that can get
me out of the dol<u>drums</u>.

Having you talk to me would really get me going. I don't know
what it is; why am I glum? I do know that I need a good talking
to. A vigor talk. And if possible, I would like there to be a
twelve minute question and answer period.

I'll pay whatever. It'll just be me and you, no one else will be
there for our pep talk. If you can't talk to me, please send me a
picture. I will look at it. That will cheer me up somewhat. But
not as much as the talk.

In the past I've had Pam Dawber (I think) pep me up and that felt
good. I felt refreshed. It works for corporations but I don't
want to spend time with a bunch of insurance salesmen. You will
be given a ride from the airport in a Mercury Topaz. (Or better).
You will also have a clean hotel room with a change of fresh
sheets.

Thanks, Ringo. You are #1. You are my favorite Beatle. Lets
talk skiffle talk.

Sincerely,

Ted L. Nancy

Ringo is
#1

560 No. Moorpark Rd. #236
Thousand Oaks, CA 91360

Feb 24, 1997

Customer Service Dept.
JERSEYMAID MILK DAIRIES
P.O. Box 3338
Los Angeles, CA 90051

Dear Jerseymaid Milk:

My dog looks just like Ringo Starr. He has the same face. His
hair under his chin look like Ringo's beard. I feed him your
nonfat milk. Whenever I show him the carton with the cow's face
on it he barks and jumps up and down until I give him some.
Everyone in town calls him the "Fifth Beatle."

Everyone that comes over says my dog looks like Ringo Starr. The
Fed Ex guy was here yesterday and he remarked, "That dog sure
looks like Ringo Starr." Then he turned a pasty white and belched
in the bushes. I had to help him in the house. He ate a pound of
grapes till he got his color back.

Can you please let me know if it is okay to feed my dog that looks
like Ringo Starr your nonfat milk on a regular basis? This is
very important as I feed it to him every day. His stool is
orange, but solid. Asparagus and broccoli does that to me. Not
Jerseymaid!

Thank you Jerseymaid people, makers of possibly the best nonfat
milk for dogs out there. I admire businesses like yours that make
products like this for dogs and humans. (If it is so).

Also, do you know anybody with a Catherine Bach look alike dog
that also drinks Jerseymaid milk? Let me know.

Very respectfully,

Ted L. Nancy
& Starkey

the
VONS.
Companies, Inc.

March 27, 1997

Ted L. Nancy
560 Norht Moorpark Road #236
Thousand Oaks CA 91360

Dear Mr. Nancy:

Thank you for your delightful letter regarding Starkey, " The Amazing Beatle Look Alike Dog" who enjoys his Jerseymaid non fat milk. We take great pride in our products and appreciate receiving feedback from our canine and human customers.

I am forwarding a copy of your letter to our Jerseymaid Dairy for their enjoyment. While we believe this is an excellent choice for Starkey to make on a daily basis, we recommend that you have him check with his vet to be sure.

Thank you for shopping with us and buying Jerseymaid products.

Sincerely,

Dotti Baker

Dotti Baker
Consumer Affairs Representative

cc: W. Kovac
      A. Scotty

The Vons Companies, Inc. • P.O. Box 513338, Los Angeles, CA 90051-1338
618 Michillinda Avenue, Arcadia, CA 91007-6300 • Telephone: (818) 821-7000

560 No. Moorpark Rd. #236
Thousand Oaks CA 91360

Sep 23, 1996

Bookings Dept.
GUTHRIE THEATER
725 Vineland Place
Minneapolis, MN 55403

Dear Bookings Dept.:

I am the leader of "THE NUDE BEATLES." We perform a condensed
history of the Beatles, but are completely naked. After ten or
fifteen minutes you forget we are nude. (Ringo wears a poncho
during Sgt. Pepper).

We are not "Unplugged." We are "The Beatles Unclothed." We
delve deeper into the history of the group than anyone ever has
before. We use tattoos and facial creams and a painter's drop
cloth.

Here's what the critics have to say:

"It's a fast paced musical exploitography."
                    ----Fritz Melk, The Alpine Barker

"I loved it."

                    ----Art Jimnet, The Nashville Reader

"I wanted to take my own clothes off."
                    ----Dottie Nitts, The Ocean City Newz

Would you like to see an audition tape of this show?   Please
write and let me know. You'll think it's the Beatles - only
naked.

Thank you,

Ted L. Nancy
The Nude Beatles

JOE DOWLING
ARTISTIC DIRECTOR

DAVID HAWKANSON
MANAGING DIRECTOR

Renting The Guthrie Theater

The Guthrie Theater is primarily used for its own presentations, however the theater is occasionally available for rent on Monday evenings throughout the theater season (May - February inclusive) and on other nights of the week during the off-season. The Theater is only available for rental for a public, paid-admission performance to other non-profit organizations, however it is available to for profit companies for private functions.

Rental Fee:

The fee for rental of The Guthrie Theater is $2000 per performance, and this rental fee generally includes the following facilities and services:

Air conditioning (or heating), lighting of public areas, clean-up of the public areas before and after performance, use of the stage auditorium, lobbies, foyers, cloak rooms, public washrooms and pay telephones.

Existing stage lighting which is defined as a general stage wash of a neutral quality is included in the rental. Any additional lighting, such as "specials", special area lighting, or additional color washes requires rental of the lighting system.

The Guthrie's sound system is included in the rental only in the event the sound requirements do not include more than the placement of a single microphone or the use of the system for a "stop and start" taped background or musical accompaniment. If additional sound is required, the renter may wish to rent The Guthrie system or choose to rent a commercial system.

Additional Charges:

The renter is required to pay additional amounts for all services and facilities not specifically included in the basic charge set forth above. The rates for the additional services and facilities are as follows:

A. Rehearsals
Rate for use of space for rehearsals on the mainstage is: $250 per four hour period, subject to availability.

VINELAND PLACE, MINNEAPOLIS, MINNESOTA 55403   (612) 347-1100

560 No. Moorpark Rd. Apt. #236
Thousand Oaks, CA 91360

Sep 23, 1996

Medical Records Dept.
MERCY HOSPITAL
3663 S. Miami Ave.
Miami, FL 33133

Dear Medical Records Dept.:

I was admitted to your hospital March 18, 1996 with a severe case
of Beatlemania. I was in the full grip of Beatlemania. I had
chills, day swells, and night twinge. I am a 57 year old white
male, 228 pounds, 5'6". (Bed wetter). I also may have had a cyst
under my armpit. I need my medical records.

When I was brought in I had a cardboard sign around my neck that
said "I Luv George" that was taken from me and I haven't seen it
since. The back of it says: "Levitz Furniture. Ottoman
Closeout." Over 100 Q-Tips were used on me. (Many in my ear).
My eyes were puffy, my underpants were on backwards, and I was
wearing a man's shorty stretch wig. (Moptop).

I was brought in at 2 a:m in an advanced state of Beatlemania,
possibly a relapse produced by the latest "Anthology" release.   I
was given a hot potato enema. (I think. Something was going on
down there).

I need my medical records. Please write and tell me how I may
proceed in getting these records. I have been in the throes of
Beatlemania twice before (once undiagnosed) but I am okay now.
Thanks for your help.

Sincerely,

Ted C. Nancy

Ted L. Nancy
"I Luv Paul"

MERCY HOSPITAL
3663 SOUTH MIAMI AVE
MIAMI FL 33133
305-285-2111

10/09/96

TED L NANCY
560 N MOORPARK RD
APT #236
THOUSAND OAKS   CA 91360

Re: NANCY, TED - Med Rec# 000000
Dear Sir or Madam:

We are in receipt of your request dated _____ for
copies of the above listed patient's medical records.

Following a thorough search or our files we are unable to
locate any records on this patient, therefore, we request
that you provide us with additional information which
would assist us in identifying the patient.

Please complete the information below, if available
(PLEASE PRINT):

- Name used at the time of treatment: _____
(NEWBORNS, please provide mother's name and sex of infant.)

- Date of Treatment: _____

- Date of Birth: _____ _____

- Social Security Number: _____

- Address: _____

- Physician's Name:_____

Please return this form to our attention. If we do not
receive this form with the additional information within
30 days from the date of this letter we will consider your
request canceled.

Sincerely,

Release of Information Desk
Health Information Management Department

560 No. Moorpark Rd. Apt #236
Thousand Oaks, CA 91360

Mar 14, 1997

Submissions
BARTENDER MAGAZINE
Foley Publishing
P.O. Box 158
Liberty Corner, NJ 07938

Dear Bartender Magazine:

I am a former long time bartender. Last week I baked a meat loaf
that looked like George Harrison. When I pulled it out of the
oven I thought to myself, "That meatloaf resembles George
Harrison." I could not eat it. Instead, I showed it to my
cleaning lady who screamed a stream of satanic obscenities, then
yelled that I was the devil and quit. (She called me Mr. Zero.
I still owe her money).

That is my story. Can I get it published? Maybe I can show you
my meat loaf that looks like the "cute" Beatle. People have
flocked to see it. It is something!

I have a picture that you would not believe. (With ketchup on
it). You will say, "He is right. That meat loaf looks like
George Harrison. You can not eat it!"

Let me know about my story. I can embellish it a little, plus
there's the picture. Plus I still work around liquor. Thank you.
I look forward to hearing from you. I love your magazine!

Sincerely,

Ted L. Nancy

Ted L. Nancy
I Like Rum!

BARTENDER

THE AUTHORITY ON BARTENDING AND ON-PREMISE

June 25, 1997

Ted L. Nancy
560 No. Moorpark Road, Apt. #236
Thousand Oaks, CA 91360

Dear Mr. Nancy:

We are in receipt of your submission to *BARTENDER* Magazine;
however, we are unable to use the material submitted and
are returning same to you.

Thank you for your interest in *BARTENDER* Magazine.

Very truly yours,

Jaclyn W. Foley
Editor

JWF:ln

Enclosure - George Harrison meatloaf

560 No. Moorpark Rd. #236
Thousand Oaks, CA 91360

Dec 6, 1996

Administrative Offices
MCCLELLAN AIR FORCE BASE
5146 Arnold Ave., Suite 1
Sacramento, CA 95612

Dear Administrative Offices,

I would like to put on a _free_ _show_ for the United States Air Force
at McClellan Air Force Base. This base is very special to me.

I would like to present my one man show "GIVE 'EM HELL, YOKO" at
your base. I am an incredible simulation. For 260 minutes I
cavort about as the woman who inspired the Beatles to pursue solo
careers.

I engage in 19 costume changes and 5 wig changes; going from long
hair to short hair in a matter of minutes. The show opens with me
(Yoko) and John (for him I use an animatronic mime doll I control
from inside my pants) reenacting the famous Toronto "sleep in." I
actually doze off for 10 minutes and the audience watches me
sleep. It is a highlight of the 260 minutes. No one leaves their
seats for snacks, bathroom visits, etc. When I wake up I am
groggy but still continue. (Early on in show).

Here is what I need from you: A bullhorn. A bathroom scale. Two
six foot forks. A fifty pound bologna. (Not fifty pounds of
bologna - no skin, please).

After the show I exhibit my autographed poncho collection in the
lobby. Please write and tell me how I go about presenting my show
FREE at your base theater for the good military at McClellan. I
look forward to hearing from you soon. Thank you.

Respectfully,

Ted L. Nancy

77MSS/DPEO
5146 Arnold Avenue
Suite #1
McClellan AFB CA 95652-1077

Ted L. Nancy
560 No. Moorpark Road
#236
Thousand Oaks, CA 91360

Dear Mr. Ted Nancy,

Civilian Training would be more than happy to avail
ourself of your services. Please provide more information
before we can make a decision on whether or not to offer
your show to our Air Force personnel.

CHET PATRAITIS
Education and Training Flight
77 Mission Support Squardron

560 No. Moorpark Rd. #236
Thousand Oaks, Ca 91360

PETE BEST
c/o Mr. Charles Rosenay
Liverpool Productions
397 Edgewood Avenue
New Haven, CT 06511   Dec 11, 1995

Dear Pete Best,

I am so glad that you are being recognized again. You were great
in the new Beatles Anthology 1 album. I was one of the
'screamers' back in the early 60's. I was always up in front and
I always screamed the loudest <u>for you</u>. I have seen you in
Liverpool and Hamburg. To me, you are the 'cute' Beatle.
I also commend you on your restraint with the Beatles going off
and becoming world famous. Most people would have gone off like a
postal worker. But you have maintained your dignity and I am glad
you are becoming respected from this latest round of Beatlemania.
(Although admittedly not as severe. I am not screaming).

You are just as much a part of history as any of the Beatles. If
you weren't in that group they may have sank. They talk about a
Beatle reunion. The other Beatles should be happy that you are
still around. With a reunion coming up you could fill in for the
missing Beatle. Why not? You are a Beatle - they need a Beatle -
it makes sense. Doesn't it? It burns me up. They keep trying to
figure out this "4th Beatle" situation when you are here!   What
gives?

I understand you are resuming your music and have an album coming
out called "Besterday." That makes me happy. You are my favorite
Beatle. YOU ARE THE CUTE ONE!!! These other Beatles should kiss
your a--! Without you they could have broken up. You kept them
going!! They should be happy you haven't gone nuts. Remember,
Ringo was the 2ND CHOICE as the Beatles drummer. You will always
be the 1ST CHOICE. That's the truth!

Please send me an autographed picture. Thanks, Pete Best. I am
your fan and can't wait until you play again. Will you be on
Anthology Two?

Sincerely,

TL Nancy

PETE BEST BAND 0151 259 5115

Pete's signature

COOPED UP

560 No. Moorpark Rd.
Suite 236
Thousand Oaks Ca. 91360

Aug 5, 1996

Administration
UNION CORRECTIONAL INSTITUTE
PO Box 221
Raiford, Fla
32083

Dear Administration Dept:

As part of my studies on human behavior, I am interested in
putting a yogurt machine in your prison and serve yogurt to all of
your death row prisoners <u>free</u> <u>of</u> <u>charge</u>.

I am convinced yogurt has a calming affect on criminals and it is
my belief that after 5 months of yogurt (and certain toppings)
even the most hardened prisoner will turn docile. I have done
this experiment on rottweilers.

I will include all popular toppings - sprinkles, nutty crunch,
gummies, and banana scrapple - which in my past experiences has
had the best effect on violent bulldogs.

If a death row prisoner thinks that he will be rewarded with a
yogurt and a topping at the end of the day he is less likely to
start a riot and burn his mattress. (Lactose intolerant
included).

I would like to set up my yogurt machine in the middle of the cell
block amongst the death row prisoners. This way they can see the
machine and know the treat is coming. But I will put it anywhere
in the prison you suggest.

I will supply the following: machine, all yogurt (swirl flavors),
myself to dispense the yogurt, and of course the popular toppings.
(Gummies will be shipped in; all others local).

I have chosen Union Correctional Penitentiary because of the
violent nature of your inmates. This works!   There is no cost
whatsoever to you at all. I will supply all yogurt AND toppings
free. I look forward to hearing from you soon.

Sincerely,

Ted L. Nancy
Ted L. Nancy

UNION
CORRECTIONAL
INSTITUTION

Governor
LAWTON CHILES

Secretary
HARRY K. SINGLETARY JR.

Post Office Box 221, Raiford, Florida 32083 • Telephone (904) 431-2000, SunCom: 831-2000

September 17, 1996

Mr. Ted L. Nancy
560 No. Moorpark Rd.
Suite 236
Thousand Oaks, CA 91360

Dear Mr. Nancy,

I have reviewed your recent correspondence regarding yogurt.

All proposals for studies on human behavior must be directed to the Office of Planning and Research in Tallahassee, Florida.

Please submit your request as follows:

Mr. Bill Bales
Planning and Research
Central Office
2601 Blairstone Road
Tallahassee, FL 32399-2500

Sincerely,

M. H. Gallemore
Assistant Superintendent of Programs

MGH/pf

cc: file

560 No. Moorpark Rd. #236
Thousand Oaks, CA 91360

MR. BILL BALES
PRISON PLANNING & RESEARCH CENTRAL OFFICE
2601 Blairstone Rd.
Tallahassee, FL 32399-2500   Dec 16, 1996

Dear Mr. Bales:

Mr. M.H. Gallemore at Union Correctional Institute suggested I
write you concerning a prison study I would like to do. I have
just finished preparing a presentation I believe beneficial for
inmates to see. I come to your prison dressed as Jesse James and
behave like Jesse and talk to the inmates of the importance of NOT
being an outlaw. How all outlaws feel sorrow and regret for their
deeds.

The performance starts at the front gate where all the prisoners
are assembled to watch me give myself up. I am then thrown in the
general population as a new prisoner in my Jesse James western
garb. I tell some more stories. I then excuse myself to go to
the bathroom and reenter as Frank James, giving a brother's
prospective of what a rotten brother I have. I come back and
argue with myself as the two of us.

I then go and change into women's clothing and come back as a
mistress of the James gang explaining the suffering of being with
this disgusting group. In a startling reenactment, I parade
around dressed in authentic frontier women's fashion mingling with
the inmates. Don't worry. I AM NOT PRETTY! (Or busty).

The performance concludes around a campfire in the prison yard
where I sing songs about bad men and everyone gets a free yogurt.

I believe this is a rehabilitative tool and am anxious to come to
your prison for my studies. I will give all results to you when I
am finished. How may I do this study at your prison? I will pay
you a fee you think is acceptable. Please write and let me know
what you would charge. I look forward to hearing from you soon.

Sincerely,

Ted L. Nancy
Ted L. Nancy

**FLORIDA
DEPARTMENT of
CORRECTIONS**

Governor
LAWTON CHILES

Secretary
HARRY K. SINGLETARY, JR.

An Affirmative Action/Equal Opportunity Employer

2601 Blair Stone Road • Tallahassee, FL 32399-2500

January 8, 1997

Mr. Ted L. Nancy
560 No. Moorpark Road #236
Thousand Oaks, CA 91360

Dear Mr. Nancy:

Your letter requesting assistance with your prison study involving your dressing as Jesse James, Frank James and a James gang mistress has been forwarded to me for response.

Your request falls into the category of a research project, and in order to be approved you would have to submit your request according to the Rules for Conducting Research (see enclosed) as defined in F.S. 33-20.007.

Before you respond, you should be aware that the general ideas expressed in your letter, such as the campfire in the prison yard and your dressing as a frontier woman and mingling with the inmates, will not be allowed under any circumstances because they are a threat to the security of the institution and your own safety.

Please send your response to my attention at 2600 Blair Stone Road, Tallahassee, FL 32399-2500. If you have questions, I can be reached at (904) 488-1801.

Sincerely,

Paula Bryant

Paula Bryant
Research Associate

PB/pb
attachments

Quality is Contagious

560 No. Moorpark Rd. #236
Thousand Oaks, CA 91360

Dec 4, 1996

Administration
FEDERAL CORRECTIONAL INSTITUTE
TUCSON
8901 S. Wilmot Rd.
Tucson, AZ 85706

Dear Prison Authorities:

I would like to perform a free show Jan 15th for your prisoners
and guards. I do a complete one man show of Johnny Cash, June
Carter Cash, and the Carter Cash sisters. I imitate 22 people! I
sing all parts and do all wig changes. I am a realistic looking
woman. As pretty as June Carter Cash. I am one sexy gal! (In
getup).

The act is two hours and 20 minutes long with full
instrumentation. (Over 3 pieces). This is a realistic sound of
the Johnny Cash - June Carter Cash San Quentin Prison show.

I want to donate my services free. There is no charge. Just a
chance to put on a great show for the inmates and guards. I want
to give back to the community. (I was given a free gum surgery by
a benevolent person and now want to repay).

I go back and forth from Johnny Cash to June Carter Cash to the
Carter Cash sisters. I sing, dance, throw marbles. I imitate the
drummer, bass player, trumpeter, and even the m.c. It is truly a
show to see! I do a flag waving, Americana, crowd rioting, horn
belching finish. The prisoners will go nuts. They'll be
screaming out of their seats. Please write and confirm my show
for Jan 15th at your institution so I just don't show up
unannounced. I can send a tape, if you'd like. Thank You.

Sincerely,

Ted T. Nancy

Ted L. Nancy
Johnny Cash, June Carter Cash, The Carter Cash Sisters
Laurie The Dog

U.S. Department of Justice

Federal Bureau of Prisons

Federal Correctional Institution

8901 S. Wilmot Rd.
Tucson, Arizona 85706

December 13, 1996

Ted L. Nancy
560 No. Moorpark Road, #236
Thousand Oaks, CA 91360

Dear Mr. Nancy:

Thank you for your recent request to perform a one-man show at the Federal Correctional Institution in Tucson, Arizona. At this time, we are unable to extend an invitation to you.

Your interest in our institution is appreciated.

Sincerely,

Robert A. Hood
Warden

560 No. Moorpark Rd.
Suite #236
Thousand Oaks, Ca 91360

Oct 17, 1996

Administrative Offices
FEDERAL CORRECTIONAL INSTITUTION
BECKLEY PRISON
P.O. Box 1280
Beaver, WV 25813-1128

Dear Prison Authorities,

I wish to donate 100 pairs of shorty pajamas to your prison.
These are perfectly good, top notch, grade A, best of the line,
choice quality, irregular, uneven, abnormal shorty pajamas (some
legs are longer).

They come in striped pale yellow. These are some of the finest
irregular shorty pajamas you will ever see.

Please write me back and tell me if your prison is interested in
this donation. I want no money.

I have an excess of shorty pajamas and I feel your penitentiary
could use them for the inmates or the guards. They are all the
same color and design, so if the inmates wear them they will all
be uniform. (Guards too). Everyone can be in these shorty
pajamas at the same time.

Please let me know so I can send them to you. Thank you and
thanks for the good job you are doing. Your inmates and guards
will look good in these pajamas.

Sincerely,

Ted L. Nancy

U.S. Department of Justice

Federal Bureau of Prisons

Federal Correctional Institution, Beckley
P. O. Box 1280
Beaver, West Virginia 25813
Telephone: (304) 252-9758

October 25, 1996

Ted L. Nancy
560 North Moorpark Road
Suite #236
Thousand Oaks, CA   91360

Dear Mr. Nancy:

This is in response to your letter dated October 17 in which you wish to donate 100 pairs of shorty pajamas to our institution.   At the present time we do not issue pajamas to inmates at this facility. Therefore, we would not have a particular need for this item. As to the possibility of donating these items to staff, this would pose an ethics issue as staff are not allowed to accept items with a value greater than $10. Therefore, I must decline your offer. Thank you for your generosity in wishing to donate these items.

Sincerely,

Keith E. Olson
Warden

560 No. Moorpark Rd. #236
Thousand Oaks, CA 91360

Feb 12, 1997

Administrative Offices
CORCORAN STATE PRISON
PO Box 9
Avenal, CA 93204

Dear Corcoran State Prison,

I wish to donate my collection of old TV guides to your prison.
It is a very nice and valuable collection. I believe your prison
would be the best place for it. The inmates would certainly like
them as they watch a lot of TV.

I'm looking at March '58 now with Ed Wynn on the cover. I also
have an '81 with Pam Dawber on the cover. Very nice.

Please tell me how I may ship these TV guides to you. They are in
order. Yesterday I looked at a '67 issue with Robert Blake. Now
they are yours. I think I may have one with Loretta Lynn
someplace in it.

Please advise. I am anxious to give this valuable gift to you.
If you want to sell them you can. They are worth quite a bit.
Especially the Michael Landon one.

Thanks for the great job you are doing with prisoners. If you
don't want to read them you can sell them and build a wing or
something. Let me know as I want to dispose of them to your
prison, Corcoran holds dear memories for me.

Respectfully,

Ted L. Nancy

DEPARTMENT OR CORRECTIONS
CALIFORNIA STATE PRISON-CORCORAN
4001 King Avenue
P. O. Box 8800
Corcoran, California 93212-8309
(209)992-8800

April 1, 1997

Mr. Ted L. Nancy
560 N. Moorpark Road #236
Thousand Oaks, CA 91360

Dear Mr. Nancy,

I am in receipt of your letter offering to donate your collection of old TV guides to the institution.

Currently, here at CSP-Corcoran, we are unable to furnish the proper storage and accountability that would be necessary for this valuable collection.

If you have any further questions, please feel free to contact me at (209) 992-6104.

Sincerely,

SYLVIA A. GONZALEZ
Community Resource Manager
Administrative Assistant/Public Information Officer (A)

560 North Moorpark Road #236
Thousand Oaks, CA 91360

Administration Offices
FEDERAL CORRECTIONAL INSTITUTE DANBURY
Route 37
Danbury, CT 06811-3099   Dec 4, 1996

Dear Administration,

I would like to perform a FREE SHOW for your prisoners and guards.
They deserve it!

I imitate the group "Santana." I play 11 different instruments
including the whistle and I imitate 9 band members plus I lip
synch and mime a 3 piece back up combo. The sound is incredible.
I call myself "SANDTANA."

I want to give back to the community. This performance WILL
include Knuckles, my otter.

I make 27 costume changes (including a sequined sleeveless vest
and a wig) under the supervision of one of your inmates. This act
is truly entertaining for the entire 180 minutes. Everyone loves
it. I bring the entire room to a rousing, hand clapping, foot
stomping, screaming and yelling (no shoving) finish. Few leave
the room to go to the bathroom or for a smoke. It is that good!

Again, there is NO COST to you. It is a FREE performance. I will
be in the Connecticut area and would like to bring this show to
you. Thank you. I look forward to hearing from you soon.

Sincerely,

Ted L Nancy

Ted L. Nancy
"Sandtana"

U.S. Department of Justice

Federal Bureau of Prisons

Federal Correctional Institution

Danbury, CT 06810

January 6, 1997

Mr. Ted Nancy
560 N. Moorpark Road
#236
Thousand Oaks, CA. 91360

Dear Mr. Nancy,

Received your letter requesting to perform a Free Show at Danbury Federal
Correctional Institution, Danbury, Connecticut.
We are interested in having your group perform for our female population.

Please contact Robert Porcaro, Recreation Supervisor at 203- 743- 6471
Extension 490. Please provide your telephone too.

Robert Porcaro, Recreation Supervisor

BLATHER

560 No. Moorpark Road
236
Thousand Oaks, CA 91360

Customer Service Dept.
HYUNDAI CARS
10550 Talbert Ave.
Fountain Valley, CA 92728   Oct 25, 1996

Dear Hyundai,

I have just been told of a FOLDING CAR that you make. This is a
standard size Hyundai that folds up and fits in your pocket when
not in use.

What a great idea! Is it heavy? I want two!

Thank you for years of possibly the best car, van, and mail truck
out there. Everyone should drive a Hyundai. I own nothing else.

When will this folding Hyundai be out? My dealer knows nothing of
it but we did go out and examine a car to see if we could fold it
up. We got the front end up and tried to bend it but that's about
it.

Please write with a picture of your new car. I will put it up on
my cork board and buy one when I get my next check. Thank you.

Sincerely,

Ted L. Nancy

Ted L. Nancy

 **HYUNDAI**

Hyundai Motor America
10550 Talbert Avenue
P.O. Box 20850
Fountain Valley, CA 92728-0850
Telephone 714 965-3000

November 18, 1996

Ted Nancy
560 N Moorpark Road #236
Thousand Oaks, CA 91360

RE: File # 347712

Dear Mr. Nancy:

Hyundai Motor America regrets to inform you that we do not manufacture a folding car that fits in your pocket when not in use. Although this sounds like a novel concept, HMA has not yet developed the technology to make such a practical vehicle.

We do appreciate your avid interest in our developing technology and hope you enjoy this small gift as a sign of our appreciation.

If you should have furthur questions, please feel free to call our 800#.

Sincerely,

E. Aquino
National Consumer Affairs
(800) 633-5151

560 No. Moorpark Rd. #236
Thousand Oaks, CA 91360

Apr 15, 1997

Building Permits
CITY OF BROKEN ARROW
City Hall
220 South 1st St.
Broken Arrow, OK 74012

Dear Building Permits:

I am writing to secure a permit to build my restaurant:
"THE RIDICULOUS BELLY." The entire restaurant will be shaped like
a large man's stomach.

I am the former owner of Imbeciles, fine Italian dining. It's
part of a chain. This is Northern Italian fare including squid
braccckkk.

Prior to that I owned Morons, home cooked Irish food. Our
specialty here was boiled potatoes, deep fried cabbage blart, and
rum strips. I also managed the Captain's Belch, seafood fare. We
specialized in fish ticks. Also, for 1 year I was day manager of
Putz's Deli. This was next door to a sewage treatment plant. We
lasted only 3 months.

In addition, I <u>may</u> open Dolt's ice cream shop with my partner
Letis Dullard. He will sign ALL papers.

Please tell me what permits I need to start building "THE
RIDICULOUS BELLY" - Broken Arrow's premier dining spot for scrod
in a cup. If I have not reached the correct department, could you
please tell me who I write to?

Thank you,

Ted L. Nancy

Ted L. Nancy

City of Broken Arrow

P.O. Box 610
Broken Arrow, Oklahoma 74013

Phone: (918) 259-8333   FAX: (918) 251-6642

April 29, 1997

Mr. Ted L. Nancy
560 North Moorpark Rd. #236
Thousand Oaks, CA 91360

Dear Mr. Nancy:

Building permits forms may be obtained from the Building Permit Department, Room 106. Permits may be issued after considerable review of all necessary forms, one at a time of course.

I am unable to begin processing your request at the present as I'm not sure if you meant your restaurant called "The Ridiculous Belly" would resemble the stomach of a large man or a large stomach on a small man. Please clarify this when you submit for a permit. A photograph showing the type of building you wish to construct would be of assistance.

If you are considering the possibility of other fine dining, I feel that Broken Arrow would very likely reject quite soundly an Italian restaurant that served squid braccckkk. But, I do think that Broken Arrow would welcome with smiles and open windows an Irish food establishment offering a menu which you describe as boiled potatoes, deep fried cabbage blart and rum strips. A Captain Belch's Seafood fare franchise, with somewhat fresh stock available, would be another fine establishment for this area.

I am somewhat puzzled by the problem you experienced with the site you chose to locate Putz's Deli, but if you would like to try it again there is a location available in South Broken Arrow.

Broken Arrow already has a very fine line of ice cream available still frozen, but please assure your partner, Letis Dullard, that Broken Arrow will do everything possible to provide multiple copies of all paperwork for an original signature.

Please be assured that not all roads lead to Broken Arrow, only the most traveled ones.

If we may be of further assistance, please contact the City Planner.

Sincerely,

Allen Stanton
Allen Stanton
Chief Building Inspector

Ted L. Nancy
560 N. Moorpark Rd. #236
Thousand Oaks, Ca 91360

Jan 3, 1996

DICK BUTKUS
C/O Vince's Baseball Cards
306 Winthrop St.
Taunton, Mass 02780

Dear Mr. Dick Butkus,

You are one mean guy. I'll bet with your name, you really got in
a lot of fights as a kid. But look what happened. You are the
toughest guy to ever play football. My last name is Nancy, so I'm
a pretty tough guy too.

As a young man, a friend of mine catered several Chicago Bears
affairs, and once let me help serve the food so I could meet some
of the players. He's retired now, so I can talk about it.

Anyway, I saved the spatula that I served you mashed potatoes
with, and would love to have you sign it.

Could you please sign it: "To Ted, Dick Butkus."

I thank you for your time, and eagerly await my personally
autographed spatula.

A Fan,

Ted L. Nancy

Ted L. Nancy

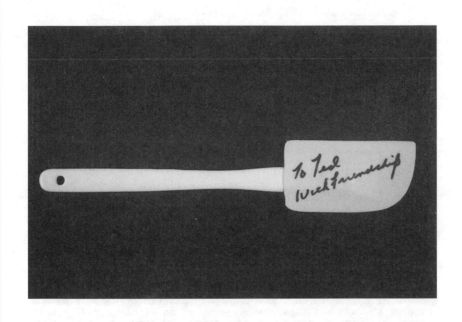

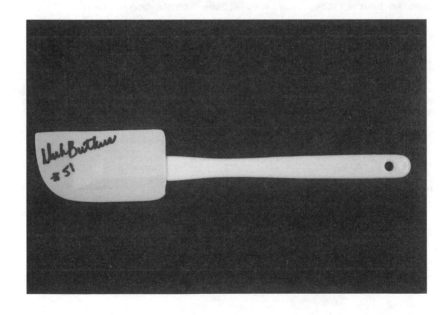

560 No. Moorpark Rd. #236
Thousand Oaks, CA 91360

Feb 18, 1997

Room Reservations
SHERATON SOCIETY HILL HOTEL
1 Dock St.
Philadelphia, PA 19106

Dear Room Reservations:

Because of my condition I am completely painted orange. I have 2
coats of Sherwin Williams orange paint on me at all times. (Only
Sherwin Williams - less gloss). I cannot be around dogs for more
than an hour as they sniff me. (Bees are dangerous too).

I need a room for the evening of Mar 20, 1997. I believe that's a
Thursday.

Is it possible to get soup as soon as I check in? I would like
sweet and sour cabbage soup the minute I arrive.

Please let me know if the March 20th date is good and how much the
rate is? Your best room, please. I am a traveler. Thank you.
And once again, I am painted orange. (Only Sherwin Williams).

Sincerely,

Ted S. Nancy

Ted L. Nancy

Sheraton Society Hill

HOTEL
PHILADELPHIA

ITT Sheraton

February 26, 1997

Dear Mr. Nancy:

At this time the rate for one person on March 20, 1997 is $165.00
plus 13% tax. Guest who check in after 4:00 p.m. must guarantee
reservation with a credit card prior to 4:00 p.m. on the date of
arrival.

Please be advised that this hotel doesn't permit guest to bring
pets with them.

Your request for sweet and sour cabbage soup can be arranged once
you have finalized your travel arrangements.

It is important that you make your reservation as soon as possible,
since the rate that was quoted is subject to availability. You can
call this hotel direct at (215)238-6000 or (888)345-7333 to make a
reservation.

Sincerely,

Arnold W. Carrington
Arnold W. Carrington
Reservations/Sales Agent

ONE DOCK STREET, PHILADELPHIA, PENNSYLVANIA 19106-3996
PHONE: (215) 238-6000 FAX: (215) 922-2709
THE SHERATON SOCIETY HILL IS OWNED BY ROUSE & ASSOCIATES - SHS, A LIMITED PARTNERSHIP, MANAGED BY THE SHERATON OPERATING CORPORATION AS ITS AGENT UNDER MANAGEMENT AGREEMENT.

560 No. Moorpark Rd. #236
Thousand Oaks, CA 91360   USA

Apr 28, 1997

TURKEY TOURIST INFORMATION OFFICE
Regional Directorate
Ataturk Cad., No: 418
Alsancak
Izmir, Turkey

Dear Turkey Tourist Information Office:

I am very much interested in camel wrestling. I have seen it on
cable. (TBS). That was something! Now I have my own camel who I
believe can beat any camel in wrestling. My camel's name is
Andrew and he is a very good wrestler. He has already beaten a
horse. He wears trunks and a cape.

Hey, are the appetizers good in Turkey? I like fried glot.

Please tell me when is the best time to come to Turkey and watch
camel wrestling? I would like to travel with Andrew but I will
come alone if my camel can not get a good rate from the airlines.
The bus company lets him travel as a senior. He looks out the
window. I have disguised him as a hairy older woman named
Margaret.

I look forward to receiving information from you regarding camel
wrestling. How much? Where? When? Why? All humps used? And
any camel souvenirs: cups, t shirts, shorts liners. Thank you,
very much.

Also, could you please tell me what airlines travels to Turkey
from the USA? Thank you.

Sincerely,

Ted L. Nancy

Number :B 17 0 TAN 4 35 06 01-12-210 -1348   I Z M I R
Ref.   :Information   25/7/1997

TED L. NANCY
560 No. Moorpark Rd. 236
Thousand Oaks,CA 91360 USA

Dear Ted Nancy,

    We're glad to have received your interesting letter and take the pleasure
in giving you some information about the points you mentioned in your letter.

    Camel Wrestling Festival takes places in the first week of January in
Selçuk-Izmir. Also in another places in the area you can find till end of February
Camel Wrestling organization but they are not regular in same dates.We beileve
that all the camels attending this festival would be so glad to meet Andrew. This
meeting would do great for the friendship between two countries as another sports
festival would.

    We searched the ways bring Andrew here. None of the airlines can accept
Andrew. Yo should look for the ways of bringing Andrew by a ship. You'll probably
have to disguise him again as a "hairy older woman named Margaret".

    We enclose a brochure about camel wrestling, which might give you an idea.
Expressing our best regards, we wish you and your camel a nice holiday in Turkey.

                                            Sincerely yours

                                            Hülya UYGUN
                                            Directress i.A.

560 No. Moorpark Rd. Apt #236
Thousand Oaks, CA 91360

Sep 23, 1996

Customer Service Department
ACME BOOT CO.
1002 Stafford St.
Clarksville, Tenn 37040

Dear Customer Service Department:

I was referred to your company for a few special order items that
I need.

Can you make a 59 inch bra?   I have large breasts and was told
that you can make a special bra for me. It's a 59 A cup. Very
narrow but still desirable to many. I was told you could
manufacture this bra out of moccasin material. Is this true?

Also, do you manufacture the Wonder Veil as I have heard?

I know you are a shoe and moccasin company and make straw footwear
and waterproof boots but I was referred to you because they said
you make special order brassieres.

I also need 50 pairs of straw waterproof moccasin boots for a
party I am giving. Who can I speak to about these straw moccasin
boots? I think the moccasin has always been the most desirable of
shoes. This party will prove it. I would prefer to have my
footwear and brassiere done by the same company.

Please write and tell me the cost and how soon my order can be
ready for these straw shoes and the big bra. Thank you for your
time. The Acme Boot Company is the best! I will tell people
that.

Sincerely,

Ted L. Nancy

Acme Boot Company
Since 1929

3 October 1996

Ted L. Nancy
560 N. Moorpark Rd. Apt #236
Thousand Oaks, CA 91360

Ted Nancy,

    We appreciate your interest in our company, however we only manufacture boots. We are unable to grant your request.

Again, we appreciate your interest.

                    Sincerely,

                  Genevieve M. Smith

                  Customer Service
                  Acme Boot Company

DAN POST®   acme®   dingo®

40 Walter Jones Blvd. • El Paso, Texas 79906 • P. O. Box 9216, Zip 79983 • (915)778-3066 • FAX (915)778-6796

560 No. Moorpark Rd. Apt #236
Thousand Oaks, CA 91360

Sep 26, 1996

Customer Service Dept.
SAN ANTONIO SPURS BASKETBALL TEAM
100 Montana St.
San Antonio, TX 78203

Dear San Antonio Spurs,

I have heard that you were changing your name to the San Antonio
Paper Towels. Why? This is a very bad idea. Probably the worst
idea I have ever heard. It is terrible. I have always liked the
name "Spurs."

I know the paper towel is strong and can "mop up" the opponent,
but I can't see myself saying "Go Paper Towels. Wipe the Lakers."

I can't remember hearing such an awful idea. It is pathetic.

Also, will you be selling San Antonio Paper Towel T-shirts?   And
what will they be made of?   What about mugs?   Give me the hours
of the gift shop so I can order memorabilia? I want a T-shirt and
a basketball and a paper towel holder.

I am wondering if the San Antonio Paper Towel logo will be on the
full line of clothing? I want some shorts!

Please tell me this name change is not so and set my mind at ease.
I am tortured. And, please give me the gift shop hours so I can
order merchandise. Thank you, San Antonio Paper Towels, you are
the team to beat.

Let me know about season tickets. I am going to move to San
Antonio in eleven weeks for a long time.

Sincerely,

Ted L. Nancy

Ted L. Nancy
You're #1 Fan

February 24, 1997

Ted L. Nancy
560 No. Moorpark Rd. #236
Thousand Oaks, CA 91360

Dear Mr. Nancy,

We are terribly sorry that you have not received our information regarding possible season tickets for the upcoming season. We are sending you some information regarding our season tickets for the 96-97 season, to give you an idea of the great opportunity the San Antonio Spurs can provide to our season ticket holders. This upcoming season's information has not yet been determined and thus we can't send you anything at this time. We will keep you in mind though, and as soon as it becomes available, we will mail it to you.

Now, in regards to our name change. I am not sure where you are getting your information, but I'm happy to inform you that the team name will continue to be "Spurs". The "Paper Towels" is a catchy name, but I don't think it would go over well with the public here in San Antonio. The people here love their spurs and would not take a name change very well. We do appreciate your interest in our organization and it's well-being.

In regards to SPURS merchandise you can call our Spurs Shop at (210) 704-6798 and order any type of Spurs memorabilia you desire. If you are ever in the San Antonio area during this season feel free to call me (210) 554-1413 and I will be glad to get you a pair of tickets to a regular season game. The Spurs are an exciting team and I know you will enjoy yourself.

Once again, thank you for you interest and I hope you tell your informant that the "Paper Towel" idea is not, and will not be considered as a possible name change.

I Love My Spurs!!

Jose Antonio Reyes
Fan Relations Coordinator

Alamodome   100 Montana   San Antonio, Texas 78203   (210) 554-7700   Fax (210) 554-7701

560 No. Moorpark Rd. #236
Thousand Oaks, CA 91360

Sep 9, 1996

Tickets
THE J. PAUL GETTY MUSEUM
17985 Pacific Coast Hwy.
Malibu, CA 90265

Dear Ticket Department,

I want to come to the J. Paul Getty Museum. I like looking at
pictures. How do I get tickets to come and see your oils?

Also...I understand you have an Italian restaurant in your museum
called the J. Paul Spagetty Restaurant? I would like to make
reservations. I like spaghetti. Is it good?

I think your Getty museum is beautiful from what I have seen in
pictures at the foot doctor's office. I understand the Spagetty
restaurant is just as beautiful. Yum.

Please send me ticket info on the museum and the hours of
operation. Also, let's make a reservation for the J. Paul
Spagetty restaurant. I like bread.

Thank you for your help. I look forward to dining there.

Respectfully,

Ted L. Nancy

Ted L. Nancy

THE J. PAUL
GETTY
MUSEUM

October 28, 1996

THE GETTY

The J. Paul Getty Museum

Research Institute for
the History of Art and
the Humanities

Conservation Institute

Information Institute

Education Institute
for the Arts

Grant Program

Leadership Institute for
Museum Management

The J. Paul Getty Trust

Ted L. Nancy
560 North Moorpark Road #236
Thousand Oaks, CA 91360

Dear Mr. Nancy:

Thank you for your interest in visiting the J. Paul Getty Museum. The Museum is open Tuesday through Sunday, 10:00 a.m. to 5:00 p.m., closed Mondays. Admission is free, however parking reservations are required. Reservations should be made 7 to 10 days in advance of your visit. Please call the Visitor Services Office at (310) 458-2003 to make your reservations.

The Garden Tea Room is a cafeteria-style eating establishment, with a menu that changes daily. They serve entrées between 11:00 a.m. and 2:30 p.m., beverages and light snacks before and after that.

I have enclosed a General Information Brochure, which has more detailed information regarding the Museum and its collections.

Thank you again for your interest. I hope you will visit the Museum soon and the new museum, opening in Fall 1997, at the Getty Center in west Los Angeles.

Sincerely,

Stephen W. Watson
Visitor Services

17985 Pacific Coast Highway, Malibu, California 90265-5799
Mailing Address: P.O. Box 2112, Santa Monica, California 90407-2112
Phone 310 459.7611 Telex 820268

560 No. Moorpark Rd. #236
Thousand Oaks, CA 91360

Sept 5, 1996

Tickets
MICKEY GILLEY THEATER
3455 W. Rte. 76
Branson, Missouri 65616

Dear Ticket Dept.,

I want to get tickets to see Boxcar Gilley. I want to come and
visit in Branson, possibly live there if the show is good. Do you
have anything for Christmas day, 1996?   I would like the 10 in
the morning show when Mr. Gilley is freshest.

I wear puffy Depends. Can I still get in?   I have lots of
problems including bloated elbows. Does that matter?   Are your
armrests padded?

Will Boxcar Gilley sing all of his favorites? I like his
spaghetti song. I saw Mr. Gilley perform in Texas, he was great!
I like his meatball tune.   Will he sing "Roomful Of Roses?"
That's my favorite. We play it at my uncle's funeral home.

Where can I get tickets?   Can you write and tell me ticket prices
and if he is doing his 10 a:m Christmas show?   Thank you very
much. Boxcar Gilley is the best!   I love his sheets.

Sincerely,

Ted L. Nancy

Ted L. Nancy

Mickey Gilley Theatre

Dear Ted Nancy-

I have received both of your letters to the Mickey Gilley Ticket Office & I do apologize for waiting this long to reply. We do no shows on Christmas Day. Our last show for 1996 is Dec 15. We start back March 1, 1997. Mickey Gilley does sing all his hit songs but I've never heard one about spaghetti Sorry.

You can get tickets by calling or the theatre & they will help you. The prices for 1997 will be $20.00

Melody Byrd

3455 West Hwy. 76 • Branson, Missouri 65616 • Telephone: (417) 334-3210 or Toll Free 1-800-334-1936 • Fax: (417) 334-3266

560 No. Moorpark Rd. #236
Thousand Oaks, CA 91360

Feb 7, 1997

BOBBY VINTON FAN CLUB
153 Washington St.
Mount Vernon, NY 10550-3541

Dear Mr. Bobby Vinton Club,

I am glad you have a fan club. You are the guy. You are the man.
I have been listening to your music for months now and it is good.
You are the KING of the world. You are better then Larry
"Hardwood Floor" Taylor. And he's good!

I play your music as LOUD as I can. My neighbor, who works until
3 in the morning as a graffiti remover then sleeps until 12, is
woken up at 7 a:m when I start playing your music. I really crank
it up. He thinks it's Roy "Ironing Board" Vinson; he's commented
to me. I eat my breakfast (Korean bark) while I listen to you
play. I have been doing this for 7 days now.

Have you ever been tickled? I mean really tickled. Tickled so
hard you belch out the name Andy? I have. Let's talk fiddle some
day when I can have visitors. Right now my body is covered with
hives. How about a picture? Of you. I will put it under my sink
and look at it when I am under there. I love you, Robert. You
are the man. The guy. Send me ANYTHING. Let's have some bark.
I want to.

How can I join your fan club?

Respectfully,

Ted L. Nancy

Ted L. Nancy

Your # 5 Fan

ARE YOU,LONELY,TIRED,RUNDOWN,OR
UNPOPULAR? DO YOU POOP OUT AT PARTIES?
THEN IF YOU'RE LIKE US ,ADMIRE
SUPERB TALENT. JOIN THE THOUSANDS OF
HAPPY PEPPY PEOPLE IN THE
BOBBY VINTON INT'L FAN CLUB.

BOBBY VINTON

Bobby Vinton Int'l Fan Club
153 Washington Street
Mt Vernon, New York 10550-3541

Bobby Vinton Fan Club
153 Washington St
Mt Vernon, NY.   10556

WESTCHESTER, NY 105
07 APR 1997

Ted E. Nancy
560 N Moorpark Road
236
Thousand Oaks, CA91260

91360-3703 08

560 North Moorpark Road #236
Thousand Oaks, CA 91360

Administrative Department
NATIONAL ARCHIVES AND RECORDS ADMINISTRATION
7th Street & Pennsylvania Avenue, NW
Washington, D.C. 20408   Dec 5, 1996

Dear National Archives:

I wish to make a valuable donation to the United States Government
for safekeeping.

I have chosen your branch of the federal government because you
are the National Archives. This should be kept by you.

My donation:

I worked in a clinic where I was able to obtain a very unusual
collectible. I have Mickey Mantle's freckles and a boil. These
are actual freckles and the boil taken off the deceased Hall of
Famer. I watched each freckle AND boil removed and discarded.
It was at this time that I retrieved my treasure. I wish to
donate them to your outstanding branch of the government where
they can be put on display and enjoyed by millions.

These are two (2) freckles 1/8th of an inch thick, 1 inch wide.
Both are caramel colored. They are definitely considered a
freckle. The boil is slightly smaller and red in color. If you
did not know what it was you would say, "That sure looks like a
boil."

Please advise on how I send you these freckles and boil. They are
fresh. I look forward to hearing from you.

Thank you,

Ted L. Nancy

National Archives

Washington, DC 20408

December 13, 1996

Ted L. Nancy
560 North Moorpark Road #236
Thousand Oaks, CA 91360

Dear Mr. Nancy:

Your letter of December 5 has been referred to me for response. The National Archives and Records Administration's statutory responsibility is limited to caring for the body of federal records created, maintained, and received in the course of conducting public business. Unless the items you propose for donation contain imbedded information regarding federal activities, the Archives could not accept your kind offer. Given the unusual nature of the donation, we recognize that your generosity holds grave ramifications beyond those normally encountered here. So even if this agency were allowed an exception to act in this instance, we are not equipped for providing the clearly specialized help you need in the matter. There must be some other institution out there equipped with adequate medical expertise to properly diagnose what kind of extended care is necessary and so we urge you to search until you find it. Good luck in your continued quest. We can all learn from the selfless gesture you are making!

Sincerely,

John A. Vernon
Chief, Education Branch (NEEE)

National Archives and Records Administration

THANK YOU FOR ACCEPTING ME

"What can I say about Ted L. Nancy? He was like a cousin to me. He lived in my mobile home. He pet my dog. He ate my sandwich."

Roy Sloppy
(Ted's Nephew)

560 No. Moorpark Rd. #236
Thousand Oaks, CA 91360

Nov 26, 1997

Customer Service
AT & T TELEPHONE COMPANY
200 N Westlake Blvd
Thousand Oaks, CA 91362

Dear Telephone Company:

I'll be moving into your city with my electronic belching machine.
I keep it on the apartment patio. Who do I contact for phone
service?

Please tell me when the installer will be there as he has to go
through my patio and will hear my machine. I don't want to get
into a shouting match with him. These belches, especially when
electronically transmitted, can get pretty loud. If I turn it up
to 7, the belches can be heard down the block.

Please tell me who I speak to for immediate service. I am moving
very soon so a quick reply would be appreciated. I need to know
who I contact for phone service. Thank you.

Sincerely,

Ted L. Nancy

Lucent Technologies
Bell Labs Innovations

Lucent Technologies Inc.
Network Systems
200 N. Westlake Blvd.
Thousand Oaks, CA 91362

December 9, 1997

Mr. Ted L. Nancy
560 N. Moorpark Road, #236
Thousand Oaks, CA 91360

Dear Mr. Nancy,

I am returning your letter, as we are no longer AT&T at this location, we are now Lucent Technologies. You local company in your area is GTE.

Sincerely,

P. J. McCormick
Office Manager

560 No. Moorpark Rd. Apt #236
Thousand Oaks, CA 91360

Dec 6, 1996

Tickets
WASHINGTON CAPITALS HOCKEY TEAM
US Air Arena
Landover, MD 20785

Dear Ticket Dept.,

I want to get season tickets for your exciting hockey team. Go
Capitals!   They are (and have always been) my favorite team. I
am moving to Washington in less then a month and this is the most
pressing issue for me - these tickets. I have a situation which I
MUST address:

I walk around with nothing but shaving cream on. That's all that
covers me. I need this for my own religious beliefs. I am of the
belief that the body is cleansed when covered in a softening type
shaving solution. This is MY religious conviction and I am
devout.

How much are season tickets? NO shaving cream will come off when
I jump out of my seat and cheer. None will evaporate. Go
Washington! If I leap out of my seat to shout, the shaving cream
will remain on me. I have done it before without incident.

Please let me know how much season tickets are and can I pick my
seat? I would like to sit in the coldest part of the arena. (Hot
areas are no good). Thank you. I look forward to a prompt
response as I MUST get my season tickets NOW. Remember, this is
for religious beliefs.

Sincerely,

Ted L. Nancy

INVOICE

December 12, 1996

Ted L. Nancy
560 North Moorpark Rd. Apt #236
Thousand Oaks, CA 91360

Attn: Ted L. Nancy

Washington Capitals: **VIP Season Tickets 1996-97 Season**
                                  Section 104, Row A, Seats 4-6

TOTAL COST: $11,160.00
PAYMENTS RECEIVED: $ 0.00
BALANCE DUE: $11,160.00
DUE THIS INVOICE (upon receipt): $11,160.00

**Please make checks payable to the Washington Capitals **
Attn:Eric Shuster

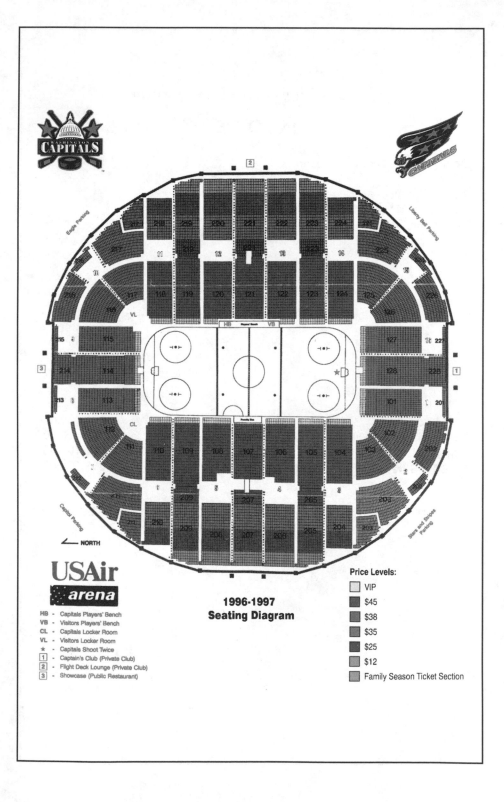

USAir arena

HB - Capitals Players' Bench
VB - Visitors Players' Bench
CL - Capitals Locker Room
VL - Visitors Locker Room
★ - Capitals Shoot Twice
1 - Captain's Club (Private Club)
2 - Flight Deck Lounge (Private Club)
3 - Showcase (Public Restaurant)

1996-1997 Seating Diagram

Price Levels:
VIP
$45
$38
$35
$25
$12
Family Season Ticket Section

560 No. Moorpark Rd. Apt #236
Thousand Oaks, CA 91360

Mar 31, 1997

Mr. Eric Shuster
Tickets
WASHINGTON CAPITALS HOCKEY TEAM
US Air Arena
Landover, MD 20785

Dear Mr. Shuster,

Thank you very much for sending me information on tickets and a
seating chart for the Washington Capital Hockey team, my favorite
hockey team. I am sorry I am so tardy in writing back but I have
been part of a religious retreat in San Diego and am now just
getting my bearings back. Whooo!

I am looking at your seating chart, and I am starting to notice
that your seating chart looks just like my dental chart. It is
very similar. Where your seats in section #204 are in the bottom
right part of my mouth, I have a deep cavity. I also have a crown
where your section #127 is, in the middle of my mouth to the
right. In addition, on the other side, where your seats in
section #11 are, I have just had a scraping done and a cap put in.
Also, section #115, near the basket, I have had gum surgery there.
Thought you'd like to know.

Please tell me if there any seats left in section 216? I have had
NO dental work done there. Also, I like to sit in the back with
my religious garb on.

Thank you. I look forward to hearing from you soon with my
Washington Capitals seating information. And I could show you my
dental chart if you want to see it. The coincidence is uncanny.
Go Capitals!

Respectfully,

Ted L. Nancy
Ted L. Nancy

560 No. Moorpark Rd.
Apt #236
Thousand Oaks, CA 91360

Aug 29, 1996

Office Of Customer Relations
ALASKA RAILROAD CORPORATION
PO Box 107500
Anchorage, AK 99501

Dear Alaska Railroad,

I am planning my first train trip. Here is my problem. I am
under 5 foot 1 inch but I have size 31 feet. This makes seating
arrangements uncomfortable. Can special arrangements be made for
my feet?

Do you think Alaska Railroad can accommodate me? Friends of mine
have raved about how accomidating Alaska Railroad can be
especially where their feet are involved. It is important that I
found out in advance before I get to the train and have to squeeze
my large feet in sideways.

If possible, I would prefer a private compartment and would pay
extra to rent one exclusively to avoid unnecessary contact to
those who might like to strike up a conversation about them. It
looks like I'm wearing clown shoes and they are noisy because
large shoes tend to slap against any floor surface. Sometimes I
need a balance bar.

Please send me your entire schedule for the United States, and
tell me how you can accommodate my feet.

Thank you. I look forward to hearing from you soon as I MUST make
my travel and feet arrangements.

Respectfully,

Ted L. Nancy

ALASKA RAILROAD CORPORATION

Corporate Address: P.O. Box 107500, Anchorage, Alaska 99510
327 W. Ship Creek Avenue, Anchorage, Alaska 99501

October 17, 1996

Mr. Ted L. Nancy
560 N. Moorpark Road
Apt. #236
Thousand Oaks, CA 91360

Dear Mr. Nancy:

Thank you for your letter requesting special accommodations for your large feet. Unfortunately, we do not have private compartments available. If you are still interested in traveling with us, please let me know and we will send you our 1997 brochure which has our 1997 schedule.

Sincerely,

Deborah L. Hansen
Director, Passenger Services

Ted L. Nancy
560 No. Moorpark Rd., #236
Thousand Oaks, Ca. USA 91360

Nov 11, 1996

MR. PRESIDENT BAILEY OLTER
Government
Pohnpei, Micronesia

Dear Mr. President Olter,

As President of Micronesia, I'm sure you get many, many letters
regarding your citizens. Yes, this is a good letter about a
great Micronesian citizen that helped me out in a big way.

I was standing in the street with a broken heel on my shoe. It
was hot and the pavement was tar-y. Anyway, my heel got stuck in
the road. I had noticed this person (he later said his name was
Kystavj or something like that) circling in his mini van with the
windows soaped over. He saw my predicament.

He pulled over and freed my tar-y heel from the hot sidewalk and
offered me a ride. At first I was hesitant. But the barrier of
the Micronesian language was broken and he gave me a ride to my
destination. This very nice gentleman from your beautiful
country fixed my heel with a staple gun. I have always wanted to
visit Micronesia. I have heard it is a beautiful land. I guess
you always have cold drinks there.

In a world where people write about all the bad things that
happen to them I am writing about something nice which happened
to me. You can be proud of your citizens. Micronesian people
are the best!!! I wish I knew this person's name.
(Koonjaminjrt or something with letters like that). He was not
from Tajikistan! Please write me and let me know you received my
letter. Thank you.

With all respect,

Ted L. Nancy
Ted L. Nancy
Future Micronesianer

NATIONAL GOVERNMENT
OF THE
Federated States of Micronesia
P. O. Box PS-53
PALIKIR, POHNPEI, EASTERN CAROLINE ISLANDS 96941
Telephone: (691) 320-2649   Telex: 729-6807   Fax: 320-2785

December 27, 1996

Ted L. Nancy
560 No. Moorpark Rd., #236
Thousand Oaks, Calif. USA   91360

Dear Nancy:

   This is in respond to your letter of November 11, 1996, in which your praised a Micronesian.

   Let me pause here for a minute and explain to you what is happening here in Federated States of Micronesia. President Bailey Olter whom you wrote to is not in this country at the moment. He is in Houston, Texas, (USA), for health reason. In the meantime, Vice President Jacob Nena is acting as the President of the country. Vice President, Jacob Nena gave me your letter to handle. My name is John A. Mangefel. I am a Liaison Man for the State Matters in this office, (President's Office, FSM).

   And now, I would like to take this opportunity to thank you for your letter of November 11, 1996. It is indeed very gratifying to receive such a letter as yours about our citizens who have migrated to your country. We are indeed very proud of such person who is promoting and "ambassadoring" good image for us in your country.

   I have tried to identify the person you mentioned in your letter through people here in the office and other people as well but we have not been able to do so. We will continue in trying to find out who is that person. In the meantime I will share your good letter with other people.

   I would like to advise and caution you though with respect to Micronesians. Like any other group of people, not all Micronesians are good people. We have our share of the so called "bad guys". I am glad you met one of the good ones. Some of us are and some are not so good.

   Again, thank you very much for writing us.

                    Sincerely yours,

                    John A. Mangefel

560 No. Moorpark Rd. #236
Thousand Oaks, CA 91360

Mar 17, 1997

Appointments
DR. EDWARD O. TERINO, M.D.
327 S. Moorpark Rd.
Thousand Oaks CA 91361

Dear Dr. Terino:

I recently lost my nose in a bad bird accident. My bowling team
teases me, but I love those guys. Here is what I would like to
know. Would it be possible to graft another part of my body and
use that as a nose? What about a toe? Could you surgically
sculpt a functioning nose (with working nostrils)?

I've heard this isn't a rare procedure in your country. (I'm new
here but have insurance and additional funds to pay for this).

Can it also work with a thumb?   My face is very important to me.
It's on my driver's license. In my line of work I use it all day
long. Your ad said to write with surgery questions. Being new in
the U.S. I have always wanted to get my nose fixed but when I saw
your ad I thought you could help me. I am willing to put down a
large deposit.

More doctors should be doing this surgery. After all, if it is
okay to make a guy out of a girl, why can't I breathe through my
big toe? Will I be able to blow my toe? Please let me know I may
come in for a consultation. I am sorry, but I am embarrassed and
would like to talk to a doctor about my nose. It is in bad shape.
Let's get my toe on my face!   Thanks for writing back and giving
me an appointment.

Sincerely,

Ted L. Nancy

Diplomat of the American Board of Plastic Surgery
Fellow of the American College of Surgeons

Aesthetic and Restorative Plastic Surgery
Restorative Surgery of the Breast

March 29, 1997

560 North Moorpark Road
#236
Thousand Oaks, CA.

Dear Ted:

Thanks for the inquiry. I wish a thumb would work for a nose, but I think that you can understand how you couldn't blow it! It is possible, however, to take the middle part of your forehead or even part of your upper arm and make a nose. It would require removing bone from your hip to build the framework. This is not a common procedure, but for accidents, it is the only way to go. It is extremely expensive, however, and takes a long time with several stages. One would have to be out of commission, so to speak or in hiding, for probably one to two years. Being new in this country, I don't think that this would serve to your advantage. If I were you, I would just tell your bowling teammates that they should love you for who you are!

Thanks again for writing.

Sincerely,

Edward O. Terino, M.D.

EOT/th

327 S. Moorpark Road • Thousand Oaks, CA 91361 • Telephone (805) 495-1043

560 No. Moorpark Rd.
Apt # 236
Thousand Oaks, CA 91360

Aug 12, 1996

CLARK COUNTY MARRIAGE LICENSE BUREAU
County Clerk's Office
200 3rd St
Las Vegas, Nev 89101

Dear Marriage License Bureau:

I am a single man interested in marrying a married couple. Can
this be performed in Las Vegas? I know Las Vegas is the marriage
capital of the world and that you can accommodate every type of
marriage.

We are simply three people that want to marry each other.
Although I am only in love with the girl, I will marry both of
them to get to her. They are already a married couple. I now
want to marry them.

How much for this? They will let me marry them but I have to do
all the legwork, so to speak. That is why I am writing to you.

Also, do you know the park hours of Wet N" Wild? I can't seem to
get them on the phone. Thank you for your help.

Please write back with info as we want to consummate our
relationship. I am ready.

Sincerely,

Ted L. Nancy

Office of County Clerk

200 South Third Street
PO Box 551601
Las Vegas NV 89155-1601

LORETTA BOWMAN
County Clerk
Commissioner of Civil Marriages

Telephones
Day: 455-3156 • Night: 455-4415
FAX: 455-4929

MARY MOSLEY
Assistant County Clerk

August 23, 1996

Mr. Ted L. Nancy
560 North Moorpark Road, Apt. 236
Thousand Oaks Ca 91360

Dear Mr. Nancy:

In reply to your correspondence, this is to advise that we are unable to accommodate the type of marriage you are requesting.

Nevada Revised Statutes states: "A male and a female person may be issued a marriage license."

We are sorry, but we are unable to provide you with the hours of Wet N' Wild.

Cordially yours,

Loretta Bowman pb

LORETTA BOWMAN, COUNTY CLERK

LB:pb

Ex-Officio Clerk of:

Eighth Judicial District Court • Board of County Commissioners • Board of Equalization
Clark County Liquor and Gaming Licensing Board • Kyle Canyon Water District
Clark County Sanitation District • General Obligation Bond Commission

560 No. Moorpark Rd. #236
Thousand Oaks, CA 91360

Nov 25, 1996

Records Dept.
CITY CLERK
305 W. 3rd St.
Oxnard, CA 93030-5790

Dear Records Dept.:

I have decided to change my name to Sinardatadadda Popppolololloppa de Del Fudgio.

I will be called "Del" to shorten my name but on all legal documents I want to be called MR. Sinardatadadda de Del Fudgio. My middle name of Popppolololloppa can be taken off all legal documents EXCEPT my gas bill.

If that name is taken I will change my name to Mitchell Silverman.

Please send me the proper forms. I am moving to Oxnard very soon. Thank you.

Sincerely,

Ted L. Nancy

Ted L. Nancy
"Del"

CITY OF
Oxnard

CITY CLERK • 305 WEST THIRD STREET • OXNARD, CALIFORNIA 93030 • (805) 385-7802
FAX • (805) 385-7806

DANIEL MARTINEZ
CITY CLERK

December 3, 1996

Mr. Ted "Del" Nancy
560 No. Moorpark Rd. #236
Thousand Oaks, CA 91360

Dear Mr. Nancy,

This letter is in response to your letter dated November 25, 1996 regarding changing your name.

The City of Oxnard does NOT provide this service. This is done through the courts at the Ventura County Government Center, 800 South Victoria, Ventura, California 93009. You will need to contact the County for the forms you request. If we can be of further assistance, please do not hesitate to contact our office.

Sincerely,

Daniel Martinez
City Clerk

pal

560 NORTH MOORPARK ROAD
236
THOUSAND OAKS, CALIFORNIA
91360

Reservations
THE RITZ HOTEL
Piccadilly, W1V 9DG
London (St James's), England   Oct 3, 1996

Dear Reservations,

I am interested in a suite at your hotel for one week, Nov 14-20,
1996. Naturally, I want the finest as I am an international
something or other.

While at your hotel, I will be greeting my business visitors
dressed as a bladder. This is a rubber costume that looks like
the human bladder. It is bloated and and veiny. It is beige in
color with the red veins running through it. It looks EXACTLY
like a bladder. You cannot tell the difference between the real
bladder and my costume.

I may have to walk through the lobby in this outfit as it is part
of my business presentation. I need to know that the security
guard will not stop me and say, "Hey, you can't walk through here
looking like a bladder!" I will have to explain to him that this
is my business costume and I have permission to walk through your
lobby dressed like a bladder. Then he will let me through so I
can hail a cab.

It is for my medical expo presentation. Do you have a suite for
the week, Nov 14-20? I look forward to hearing from you and
getting clearance for my bladder outfit. Thank you.

Sincerely,

Ted L. Nancy

Ref: TOC/kt

9th October 1996

Mr Ted L Nancy
560 North Moorpark Road, #236
Thousand Oaks, CA 91360
USA

Dean Mr Nancy.

Thank you for your facsimile which was addressed to our Reservations Department.

I regret to advise that whilst your proposal is very novel, we do not really feel that it would be appropriate given the restriction we place on dress within the hotel. I am sure you will understand that having requested our guests wear jackets and ties and not to wear jeans and training shoes, if we were to allow a costume to be worn we would be severely criticised.

Thank you, however, for having considered The Ritz.

Yours sincerely

Tom O'Connell
General Manager

560 North Moorpark Road
#236
Thousand Oaks, California 91360 USA

MR. TOM O'CONNELL
General Manager
THE RITZ HOTEL
150 Piccadilly, London
W1V 9DG England   Mar 27, 1997

Dear Mr. O'Connell,

Thank you for answering my letter regarding accomodations for
myself in my bladder outfit. I still need a suite for 1 week as
my conference has been rescheduled for May 2-7, 1997.

And thank you for explaining to me that a man dressed as a bladder
would be out of place in your luxury hotel. Oh my goodness, I had
no idea you thought I would come to your fine hotel dressed just
as a bladder. Of course, I realize that you have a dress code
there. I will wear a tie, starched shirt, and hard shoes over my
bladder clothing. In essence, I will be dressed as a formal
bladder. I am sure that this will be acceptable. (I am hoping).
I have worn this clothing in front of the president before. (At a
mattress shop opening at the airport).

I will leave substantial gratuities in this outfit and I will
behave in a dignified manner. My outfit will NOT cause a
disturbance once the guests have seen me a few time relaxing in
the lobby and conducting business in this stretch rubber organ
suit. They will not even notice me anymore. Oh sure a few will
say, "Who is that man dressed like a bladder relaxing for hours in
the lobby?" "Oh, him? He's there a lot."

So, can you tell me if you have a suite available for the week of
May 2-7, 1997? And can I get a corporate rate? This is a
conference. Thank you. I look forward to your reply.

Sincerely,

Ted L. Nancy
Ted L. Nancy

Ref: GRCS/kt

2nd April 1997

Mr Ted L Nancy
560 North Moorpark Road #236
Thousand Oaks, California 91360
USA

Dear Mr Nancy,

Thank you for your letter of 27th March which was addressed to Mr O'Connell regarding the availability of a suite for 2nd-7th May 1997. Mr O'Connell left The Ritz in November last year to return to Ireland and I am therefore answering on his behalf.

I am afraid that we are not able to help you on this occasion. The week of 2nd-7th May is extremely busy and we have no suites available at that time.

Yours sincerely

Giles Shepard
Managing Director

The Ritz, London

150 Piccadilly, London W1V 9DG
Telephone (0171) 493 8181   Facsimile (0171) 493 2687
The Ritz Hotel (London) Ltd. Registered in England No 64203C. VAT Registration No 420 4790 73

560 No. Moorpark Rd. #236
Thousand Oaks, Cal 91360

Aug 7, 1996

Customer Satisfaction Dept.
ALBERTO VO 5 SHAMPOO
Alberto Culver USA
Melrose Park, Ill 60160

Dear Alberto VO 5 Shampoo,

I shampoo my alligator in your shampoo. He likes strawberry. I
raise alligators and lizards and perch.   Only the alligator likes
your strawberry shampoo. Sadly, the others turn their nose up at
it when I put the bottle under it.

But my alligator goes wild when I put the shampoo on him. He
closes his eyes tight and enjoys every moment

If I stop he opens his eyes and waits for more shampooing.

Do you make other products for alligators? Please let me know.
Have you ever heard of this? I need to know that I am not crazy
and my alligator is definitely not crazy. Tell us.

If you want a picture I can show you one with lather on his head
and his eyes closed tight. Thanks. Write me so I can show others
in the breeding area that your company cares where their shampoo
goes. And let me know if you want to see that picture. It is
something to see - a 12 foot alligator with your lather on his
head. He likes it!

Thank You,

Ted Nancy
& Mark

ALBERTO-CULVER USA, INC.

October 1, 1996

Ted Nancy
560 No. Moorpark Rd. #236
Thousand Oaks, CA 91360

Dear Mr. Nancy:

Thank you for your letter regarding your alligator's use of
Alberto VO5 Strawberry & Cream Shampoo. It's always a pleasure to
hear from a satisfied customer.

Alberto VO5 Shampoos and Conditioners are especially developed for
human hair, with a blend of ingredients that moisturize and
beautify hair, giving it exceptional body. VO5's triple
conditioning formula offers three conditioning benefits: provides
essentail moisture and locks it in, strengthens and protects
during wet combing and restores precious moisture and vitality,
leaving hair soft.

Alberto VO5 Shampoo ingredients are combined so the shampoo has a
PH balance which falls between 3.9 - 6. It is not uncommon for
Alberto-Culver Shampoos, and also those of our competitors, to
have a PH in the range between 4.0 - 6.0. This range includes the
PH values dermatologists consider to be the "acid mantle" of human
skin. By that they mean that this is in the normal PH range of
the skin.

Shampoos, as well as other skin and hair products that are
intended for skin application, are intentionally PH adjusted so as
not to interfere with the native PH level of the skin.

The PH level also effects the shampoo's ability to neutralize or
remove residues of hair treatment products. Therefore, it may be
necessary for a particular shampoo formula, such as VO5 Baby
Shampoo, to have a slightly higher (5.5) acid level in order to
clean the hair gently and naturally.

We hope this information is helpful. We have heard many stories
of using Alberto VO5 Shampoo on dogs and cats, but yours is the
first of an alligator's use. Please note Alberto Culver has never
tested Alberto VO5 products on animals, since it is only intended
for human use.

Sincerely,

Mary Alexander
Manager
Consumer Relations

MARK '94

MARK NOW

EPILOGUE

560 No. Moorpark Rd. Apt. #236
Thousand Oaks, CA 91360

Mar 22, 1997

Customer Service
TIMOTHY FIDGE SPOON COMPANY
27855 El Camino Real
Palo Alto, CA 94301

Dear Timothy Fidge Spoon Company,

I want to tell you that I like my spoon. It is the best spoon I
have ever used. Better than my fork. I am very happy with this
spoon. I eat the following foods with my spoon: melon chunks,
gelatin, cereal, yams, gravy, corn, pie filling, grapefruit.

Others have commented that this is certainly a nice spoon but I
tell them that it's mine. They will have to get their own.

I would like you to thank everybody there that's responsible for
my spoon. I'm sure many people worked on it and now they should
be thanked. People should know that they're just not looking at
spoons all day. That others appreciate them. Would you thank
everybody for me?   I would appreciate that. Thank you.

I will continue to use my spoon on the following: squash, peas,
cantaloupe meat, pudding, gumbo, chili, sandwich slop.

You make a good spoon! Probably the best. I tell everyone that.
That the Timothy Fidge Spoon Company makes the best spoon out
there! Please thank everyone at your company for me. Would you
let me know they were thanked? Thank you. I understand you
started out as a small toothpick plant in Maine in the year 1271.
I use small toothpicks all the time.

Respectfully,

Ted L. Nancy

Ted L. Nancy

ℑimothy Fidge & Co.
custom jewelers

MEMBER
(AGS)
AMERICAN GEM SOCIETY

April 16, 1997

Ted L. Nancy
560 N. Moorpark Road ~ Apt 236
Thousand Oaks, CA 91360

Dear Mr. Nancy,

On behalf of the employees of Timothy Fidge Spoon Company, I would like to take this opportunity to thank you for your recent letter. We were pleased to learn that you were so happy with your spoon, and that you have found so many uses for it. I am sure over time you will find that there are so many other foods, in addition to the ones you mentioned, that you will be able to eat with your spoon.

Per your request, I am letting you know that I personally thanked the employees of Timothy Fidge Spoon Company for your spoon. I would like to know who in particular assisted you with your order. Do you recall the name of the Timothy Fidge employee who helped you with your spoon. Was your order placed in person or by telephone?

Because of the distance between the location of Timothy Fidge Spoon Company and your residence we are curious to know just how you heard about us. Was it through some form of advertising or maybe word of mouth?

We would also like to know how you heard about us starting out as a small toothpick plant in Maine in the year 1271. Since you mentioned you use small toothpicks all the time, we would be happy to make you a solid gold toothpick. Just let us know if you would prefer the rounded style or flat style.

At Timothy Fidge Spoon Company, we pride ourselves on quality. It is always gratifying when a customer can identify true quality in a piece that we have produced. We appreciate your comments, and look forward to working with you on any future custom orders.

Sincerely,

Marilyn Fidge
Timothy Fidge Spoon Company

27 Town and Country Village, Palo Alto, California 94301 (415) 323-4653